**BIOMES OF THE EARTH**

# TUNDRA

Peter D. Moore

Illustrations by
Richard Garratt

**CHELSEA HOUSE**
PUBLISHERS
An imprint of Infobase Publishing

**Tundra**

Chelsea House
An imprint of Infobase Publishing
132 West 31st Street
New York NY 10001

**Library of Congress Cataloging-in-Publication Data**
Moore, Peter D.
  Tundra / Peter D. Moore; illustrations by Richard Garratt.
    p. cm. — (Biomes of the Earth)
  Includes bibliographical references (p.   ) and index.
  ISBN 0-8160-5325-1
  1. Tundra ecology—Juvenile literature. 2. Tundras—Juvenile
literature. I. Garratt, Richard, ill. II. Title. III. Series.
QH541.5.T8M66 2006
577.5'86—dc22                                    2005035618

Chelsea House books are available at special discounts when purchased in bulk quantities for businesses, associations, institutions, or sales promotions. Please call our Special Sales Department in New York at (212) 967-8800 or (800) 322-8755.

You can find Chelsea House on the World Wide Web at http://www.chelseahouse.com

Text design by David Strelecky
Cover design by Cathy Rincon
Illustrations by Richard Garratt
Photo research by Elizabeth H. Oakes

Printed in China

CP Hermitage 10 9 8 7 6 5 4 3 2 1

This book is printed on acid-free paper.

# CONTENTS

# PREFACE

Earth is a remarkable planet. There is nowhere else in our solar system where life can survive in such a great diversity of forms. As far as we can currently tell, our planet is unique. Isolated in the barren emptiness of space, here on Earth we are surrounded by a remarkable range of living things, from the bacteria that inhabit the soil to the great whales that migrate through the oceans, from the giant redwood trees of the Pacific forests to the mosses that grow on urban sidewalks. In a desolate universe, Earth teems with life in a bewildering variety of forms.

One of the most exciting things about the Earth is the rich pattern of plant and animal communities that exists over its surface. The hot, wet conditions of the equatorial regions support dense rain forests with tall canopies occupied by a wealth of animals, some of which may never touch the ground. The cold, bleak conditions of the polar regions, on the other hand, sustain a much lower variety of species of plants and animals, but those that do survive under such harsh conditions have remarkable adaptations to their testing environment. Between these two extremes lie many other types of complex communities, each well suited to the particular conditions of climate prevailing in its region. Scientists call these communities *biomes*.

The different biomes of the world have much in common with one another. Each has a plant component, which is responsible for trapping the energy of the Sun and making it available to the other members of the community. Each has grazing animals, both large and small, that take advantage of the store of energy found within the bodies of plants. Then come the predators, ranging from tiny spiders that feed upon even smaller insects to tigers, eagles, and polar bears that survive by preying upon large animals. All of these living things form a complicated network of feeding interactions, and, at the base of the system, microbes in the soil are ready to consume the energy-rich plant litter or dead animal flesh that remains. The biome, then, is an integrated unit within which each species plays its particular role.

This set of books aims to outline the main features of each of the Earth's major biomes. The biomes covered include the tundra habitats of polar regions and high mountains, the taiga (boreal forest) and temperate forests of somewhat warmer lands, the grasslands of the prairies and the tropical savanna, the deserts of the world's most arid locations, and the tropical forests of the equatorial regions. The wetlands of the world, together with river and lake habitats, do not lie neatly in climatic zones over the surface of the Earth but are scattered over the land. And the oceans are an exception to every rule. Massive in their extent, they form an interconnecting body of water extending down into unexplored depths, gently moved by global currents.

Humans have had an immense impact on the environment of the Earth over the past 10,000 years since the last Ice Age. There is no biome that remains unaffected by the presence of the human species. Indeed, we have created our own biome in the form of agricultural and urban lands, where people dwell in greatest densities. The farms and cities of the Earth have their own distinctive climates and natural history, so they can be regarded as a kind of artificial biome that people have created, and they are considered as a separate biome in this set.

Each biome is the subject of a separate volume. Each richly illustrated book describes the global distribution, the climate, the rocks and soils, the plants and animals, the history, and the environmental problems found within each biome. Together, the set provides students with a sound basis for understanding the wealth of the Earth's biodiversity, the factors that influence it, and the future dangers that face the planet and our species.

Is there any practical value in studying the biomes of the Earth? Perhaps the most compelling reason to understand the way in which biomes function is to enable us to conserve their rich biological resources. The world's productivity is the basis of the human food supply. The world's biodiversity holds a wealth of unknown treasures, sources of drugs and medicines that will help to improve the quality of life. Above all, the world's biomes are a constant source of wonder, excitement, recreation, and inspiration that feed not only our bodies but also our minds and spirits. These books aim to provide the information about biomes that readers need in order to understand their function, draw upon their resources, and, most of all, enjoy their diversity.

# ACKNOWLEDGMENTS

I should like to record my gratitude to the editorial staff at Chelsea House for their untiring support, assistance, and encouragement during the preparation of this book. Frank K. Darmstadt, executive editor, has been a constant source of advice and information, and Dorothy Cummings, project editor, has edited the text with unerring skill and impeccable care. I am grateful to you both. I should also like to thank Richard Garratt for his excellent illustrations and Elizabeth Oakes for her perceptive selection of photographs. I have also greatly appreciated the help and guidance of Mike Allaby, my fellow Chelsea House author. Thanks to my wife, who has displayed a remarkable degree of patience and support during the writing of this book, together with much needed critical appraisal, and to my daughters, Helen and Caroline, who have supplied ideas and materials that have enriched the text. I must also acknowledge the contribution of many generations of students in the Life Sciences Department of the University of London, King's College, who have been a constant source of stimulation and who will recall (I trust) many of the ideas contained here. Thanks are also due to my colleagues in teaching and research, especially those who have accompanied me on field courses and research visits to many parts of the world. Their work underlies the science presented in this book.

# INTRODUCTION

Few words conjure up such bleak images as the word *tundra*. If asked to write down the ideas that come into their heads on hearing the word, most people would probably include: cold climate; unproductive, treeless, bare landscapes; and little sign of life, with a total lack of human habitation. There is a measure of truth in these ideas, but they are far from the whole truth. In fact, summer days in the tundra can be extremely warm, and for short periods the vegetation can be very productive. Although low in diversity, the tundra is rich in living organisms. Trees are present, but they tend to grow only to knee height, and humans manage to make a living in these regions despite the rigors of the tundra winter.

## What is the tundra?

The word *tundra* is derived from the language of the Sami (Lapps) in northern Finland, Sweden, and Norway, who inhabit this open landscape. The tundra is a biome that is associated with the high, polar latitudes, occupying land that is farthest from the tropical, equatorial regions. But it is also found on the summits of the world's high mountains, which experience a similar climate of low average annual temperature. Tundra vegetation is low and open, for the strong winds and icy conditions of winter are too severe for the growth of tall trees, whose buds would be blasted by airborne ice particles if they were to extend far above the surface of the ground. Low shrubs and dwarf trees survive, however, forming a bushy cover of vegetation lying close to the ground. In some locations, especially on exposed, rocky ridges, even this amount of vegetation cannot survive, and bare rocks or gravel ridges are almost devoid of plants apart from a compressed cover of scale-like lichens or small cushions of mosses that find shelter in the crevices. Within these patches, invertebrate animals such as insects and nematode worms eke out a living and serve as food for predators, particularly the birds that arrive in the area to breed during the summer.

Below the surface of the ground, the life-bearing soil is shallow because the deeper layers (the permafrost) are permanently frozen, and neither the roots of plants nor the animals of the soil can penetrate into this zone. The upper layers of the soil also freeze during the winter but defrost and become active with life during the summer season. This is another reason why tall trees cannot survive in tundra: Trees need deep roots to give them stability and an assured supply of water, but due to the permafrost the available soil is too shallow for tree roots to flourish.

When temperatures are low and water is frozen, plant roots are no longer able to obtain it from the soil, so water supply can actually be a problem in the tundra, especially the polar tundra where precipitation (snow and rainfall) is low. The well-drained ridges in particular suffer because they may also become very dry in summer and plants can find difficulty in obtaining enough water to survive. In the lower-lying areas between ridges, on the other hand, water accumulates and creates wetlands that provide breeding grounds for invertebrates and waterbirds during the summer months. Often these wetlands develop patterns over their surfaces that are very apparent from the air, giving the appearance of marble or of honeycombs on the surface of the ground.

The wildlife of polar tundra reaches its peak of activity in the brief summer, when the vegetation is at its most productive. The resident mammals, which may include seals, polar bears, arctic foxes, or, in the southern polar regions, penguins, enter their breeding season. Other animals arrive from the lower latitudes where they have spent the unfavorable winter season, among them the caribou migrating northward from the coniferous forest zone, and birds that come to take advantage of the abundant supply of insect life and the long days in order to feed themselves and their hungry offspring.

Away from the poles, on the summits of high mountains even in the tropical zone, another tundra habitat can be found. This is called alpine tundra. The word *alpine* is taken from the Alps, the high mountains of central Europe, but geographers and ecologists use it to refer to all high mountain habitats. Alpine tundra has many similarities to the polar tundra: It is treeless, annual average temperature is low, and the more mobile animals may migrate into the zone during the productive summer months. Many of the plants found in alpine tundra are also found in the polar tundra, which shows how similar conditions are. But there are also some important differences. Near the equator (such as on the mountains of East Africa, latitude 0°) there is very little difference between summer and winter conditions, but the contrast between the seasons becomes increasingly extreme the farther the location lies from the equator. The difference between summer and winter becomes greater moving northward through the Himalayas (30°N), Sierras (40°N), Alps (48°N), Scotland (60°N), and Brooks Range, Alaska (70°N). The winters are increasingly long and cold when the mountains lie closer to the poles. (These mountain ranges are shown in the illustration on page 20.) It is not only in the seasonal climate that differences in these montane tundra habitats are found, however; there is also a contrast in the daily range in the temperature of alpine tundra habitats. In tropical mountains, and even in the temperate mountains that lie closer to the equator, such as the southern Sierra Nevada in California, there is a great difference between daytime and nighttime temperatures; this is less marked as one moves toward the poles. Alpine tundra regions also tend to have higher precipitation (particularly snowfall) than the polar tundra, and this often accumulates, leading to the formation of packed ice masses, the glaciers. These climatic differences as well as the isolation of alpine tundra, which has led to evolutionary changes, mean that alpine and polar tundra differ from one another in their physical conditions and consequently in many of the plants and animals that occupy them.

Tundra, therefore, is quite a widespread and varied habitat. It has developed in response to extreme conditions, particularly the impact of intense cold. It contains wildlife that is not as diverse as that of the lowland Tropics but is of great biological interest simply because it is capable of withstanding or avoiding the stresses to which it is exposed. Highly adapted plants and animals are found here that have evolved distinctive mechanisms for coping with harsh conditions by modifying their structure, their biochemistry, or their behavior. The tundra is, therefore, a living laboratory in which biologists and ecologists can study the way in which nature deals with intense challenge.

## Why is tundra important?

The most frequently used argument for preserving a habitat is the value of its biological diversity, or biodiversity. In the range of living organisms found within a biodiverse habitat there resides a great bank of genetic information locked within the cells of animals and plants, and the genes they contain may be of importance to humans in the future. Within these genes lie the keys to food production and drug manufacture that may one day be vital to human survival. To lose any plant or animal because of extinction is a mistake that is irreversible and so is best avoided. It is relatively easy to argue for the importance of the tropical rain forest because of its immense biodiversity. But what of the tundra? It is a general principle of biogeography that as one moves from the equator to the poles, there is an overall reduction in biodiversity. The tundra is lower in biological diversity than any other biome, even lower than the hot deserts. There are fewer species of plants, insects, birds, and mammals in this biome than in any other.

Does this mean that the tundra is of little importance in the conservation of biodiversity? The answer is no. Tundra is important because the organisms that are found in this biome are entirely different from those of the Tropics. There may not be as many species, but the species that occur are not the same ones that are found in the rain forest. Moreover, they are also species that have developed under extreme pressures, and this means that their structure and their biochemistry are very distinctive and well adapted to these conditions. The genes that control these traits could well be useful to humans in the future, so these species also need to be conserved. If humans need to improve crops, or domesticated animals, or forest trees for use in cold climates, then the genes contained in the tundra wildlife may hold the clue to such developments. The mechanisms by which warm-blooded animals can hibernate beneath the snow, or by which plants can withstand the drought or the cold of a tundra winter, may one day be vital to medicine and agriculture, respectively.

Another reason why tundra is important is the fact that it lies in remote locations. Tundra habitats are very useful as monitoring stations of relatively undisturbed and unpolluted habitats, so they can be used to check the general state of health of the world. The discovery in the 1950s of the pesticide DDT in Antarctic penguins, for example, provided an early warning of the way in which this harmful material had found its way even into the most remote parts of the planet. The shock generated by information of this sort helped persuade governments to ban the use of this particularly persistent toxin. Likewise, the discovery of a hole in the ozone layer of the stratosphere (a layer of the Earth's atmosphere) over the Antarctic and, more recently, the Arctic has emphasized the importance of the polar regions in the functioning of the entire planet. The behavior of the polar atmosphere needs more research, and the impact of these processes on living plants and animals is best studied in the tundra biomes.

Besides these quantifiable benefits provided by this biome, people also gain much pleasure from the tundra in leisure and recreational activities. Ecotourism that takes parties into the high Arctic and Antarctic is now both popular and profitable. Parties of tourists find relaxation, education, and pleasure in watching the calving of icebergs in Alaska, the breeding flocks of emperor penguins in the Antarctic, or the wandering polar bears of Hudson Bay. Many other people who will never be able to visit these regions of the world enjoy the images and information about them now available from books, magazines, and television. Tourism is also associated with the alpine tundra habitats of the world. Besides the seashore, mountains are for many the most attractive environment for rest and relaxation, but the pressures that humans place upon this fragile habitat can be harmful to its wildlife, so care is needed in the development of tourism.

If humans are to take care of the tundra, then they must be able to understand how it works, which is the subject of this book. There are many questions that need to be answered in order to understand the way the tundra functions, and these will be considered in the course of the book. Where are the tundra habitats found in the world, and what are the environmental factors that control the distribution of this biome? In lands that often lie beneath ice and snow, what is the impact of glaciers upon the geology of the landscape? What unusual features about the tundra ecosystem enable it to function under climatic stress? How do plants and animals manage to make a living in such a difficult environment? What kinds of plants and animals survive here, and what are the adaptations that make them successful? How long has the tundra existed on Earth, and how has its extent varied in the past?

The tundra has a history of human interaction, and people will continue to use the tundra, exploiting its mineral wealth and enjoying its grandeur. But the impact of past and present human activities on the biome must be calculated, and future human impact must be controlled. The tundra is a unique habitat that deserves to be actively conserved, and the final section of the book will explore how this may be done. The future of tundra lies in human hands.

# CHAPTER 1

# GEOGRAPHY OF THE TUNDRA

Geography is the study of the Earth and includes the way in which landforms and living things are distributed over the surface of the Earth, what factors have caused their distribution, and how the world came to contain the forms now found here. Geography can teach people much about the tundra biome, including the parts of the world in which it is found and the reasons why it has this distribution pattern.

## Where is the tundra biome found?

Tundra ecosystems are found only under very cold conditions and these are most typically associated with the polar regions. Perhaps surprisingly, neither the North Pole nor the South Pole is occupied by tundra vegetation. At the North Pole, the reason for this is that the pole lies far from solid land in the middle of the Arctic Ocean. In winter the sea is largely frozen so that the pole can be reached on foot, but the pack ice becomes unstable in the summer and partially breaks up. The lack of land in the immediate vicinity of the North Pole means that there is no true tundra vegetation. The South Pole, on the other hand, does lie on a large continental landmass, but the bulk of the continent is occupied by a permanent ice cap, so once again tundra vegetation is absent from the pole and its surroundings. The South Pole actually lies two miles above the land surface, perched on top of this massive thickness of ice. In both situations, therefore, the tundra habitat forms a ring around the poles at some distance from them. Tundra is also present at other places on the Earth's surface where conditions are sufficiently cold, particularly on high mountaintops often far from the polar regions. Here also, the very highest peaks are bare of any vegetation and the packed ice of glaciers may occupy the valleys

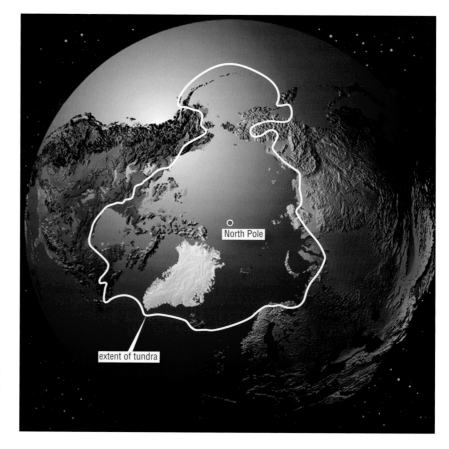

North Pole

extent of tundra

*The extent of the Arctic tundra. South of this line, forest becomes increasingly abundant.*

at high altitude. Below this ice zone lies the alpine tundra, again forming a ring between ice and forest.

The map above shows the extent of the tundra region around the North Pole. It occupies the coastal region of Alaska and the Aleutian Islands and the northern parts of Canada, sweeping south to include the coast of Hudson Bay, the northern tip of Newfoundland, and the whole of Greenland and Iceland. It includes the northern coastal strip of Norway and the northern edge of Russia, sweeping south again in the northern Pacific to skirt the Bering Sea. In Antarctica, the great extent of the ice cap, much of which is situated on land below sea level, restricts tundra to isolated fragments along the coastal regions and islands, especially at the tip of the Antarctic Peninsula.

Alpine tundra is, of course, more scattered over the face of the Earth, wherever high mountains are to be found, from the Arctic to the equator. In the Americas, alpine tundra is found most abundantly in the mountain ranges of Alaska; in the Rockies, Cascades, and Sierra Nevada in the west of North America; and down the Andes chain of western South America. In Europe, the mountains of Scandinavia and Scotland bear tundra vegetation, as do the Alps and Pyrenees. In Asia there are high mountains, the Caucasus, to the west of the Caspian Sea, but the continent is dominated by the massive Himalayas, the great mountain plateau of Tibet, and the ranges running eastward through Mongolia to the northeastern regions of Russia. In Africa the Atlas Mountains lie on the north and the Drakensberg Mountains in the far south; between them are several very high mountains almost on the equator in East Africa, and also in Ethiopia. Other isolated high mountains are scattered around the world, as in Mexico and Japan.

The polar tundra, by definition, occurs far from the equator in what are known as the high latitudes. The high latitudes are given this name because the lines of latitude that encircle the world are numbered from the equator, which has

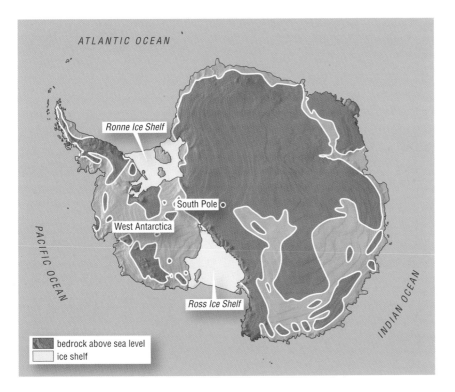

Map of the Antarctic continent, showing the extent of the ice sheet and the distribution of bedrock above sea level beneath the ice. Some of the ice sheet lies directly on bedrock below sea level. The ice shelves consist of floating permanent sea ice.

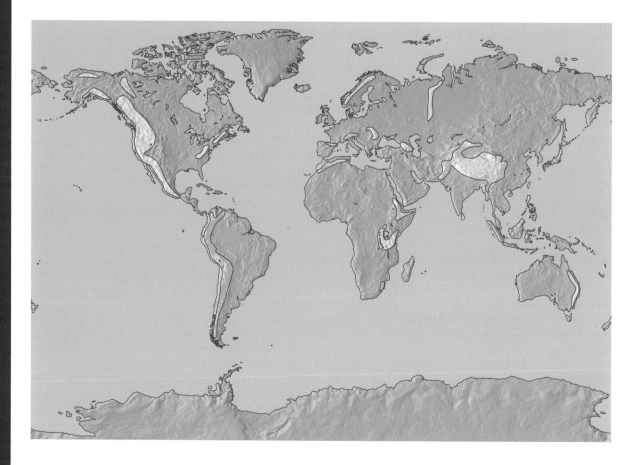

*The distribution of the main mountain ranges of the world. The two major ice sheets and the main regions of mountain glaciers are also shown.*

a latitude of 0 degrees. A cross section through the Earth would show that the North and South Poles are at right angles to the line of the equator, so these have latitudes of 90°N and 90°S, respectively. Between the equator and the poles, the angles of the lines of latitude lie between 0° and 90° with the higher values being closer to the poles; hence the polar regions are referred to as the high latitudes and the equatorial regions as the low latitudes. Mountains occur both at high and low latitudes, as shown in the illustration on this page and also in the illustration on page 20.

## What factors determine tundra distribution?

Most of the world's biomes, such as rain forest, desert, and savanna grassland, occupy distinct zones around the world, usually lying within a particular range of latitudes. The tundra biome is evidently different, being found at high latitudes but also scattered through the low latitudes. There must be certain factors in common between the polar regions and the high mountain habitats in locations closer to the equator. All of the major biomes, including those listed previously, are ultimately controlled by climate, so it is reasonable to begin an investigation into tundra distribution by looking at climatic factors.

The most obvious feature that all areas of tundra, both polar and alpine, share is their cold climate. High latitude and high altitude both have low average annual temperatures but, as will become clear, for different reasons. In general all tundra habitats, whether polar or alpine, have average annual temperatures below 25°F (−4°C). Low temperature is important in maintaining the tundra biome because it restricts tree invasion. When the overall temperature is above this critical limit, tree seeds, such as birch, spruce, and pine, are able to germinate and establish themselves. Forests of coniferous and deciduous trees usually mark the edge of the polar tundra that lies closest to the equator, while permanent ice or ocean determines its poleward edge. In the case of alpine tundra, forest similarly forms a lower altitudinal boundary to the extent of the biome. So tundra exists because the climate is too cold to permit forest growth.

The annual average temperature, however, is not an adequate index of the general climate of tundra regions. A site with warm summers and cold winters may have the same average temperature as a location that is cool throughout the year, so the seasonal variation in temperature needs to be considered. Also important for vegetation is the length of the growing season; a very short growing season, even if warm, may be inadequate for forest growth and therefore may encourage the development of tundra. But even tundra vegetation has its limits and needs some time clear of snow in order to photosynthesize and build up a store of energy.

There are other factors apart from cold that play a part in the maintenance of the tundra. Among these, high winds are particularly important. The open expanses of the polar tundra and the high peaks and ridges of the alpine tundra are prone to high winds, sometimes bearing particles of ice suspended in the fast-moving air, and this can be extremely damaging to vegetation if it projects far above the surface of the soil. Shrubs are constantly trimmed by ice-blasting, and taller trees are quickly eliminated.

The soils of the tundra, both polar and alpine, may be frozen for much of the year or buried beneath the snow. The germination of seeds is hindered by snow burial and the development of roots is restricted by frost, so tree invasion is prevented. The soils of the tundra regions will be considered later (see "Soil formation in the tundra," pages 55–57).

Water availability may not seem a problem in lands of ice and snow, but the cold conditions can make it difficult to obtain. Vegetation needs a reliable supply of water because evaporation is constantly removing water from leaves, so when cold makes water difficult to obtain, the plant suffers. This is particularly true of plants with large leaves, including many trees.

So, the two main climatic factors that influence plants and animals are temperature and water. The graph below represents the occurrence of the tundra biome with respect to these factors as compared with the other major biomes. Here the annual precipitation is shown on the vertical axis and the annual temperature on the horizontal axis. Biomes that need high rainfall and high temperature, such as tropical forest,

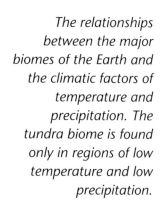

*The relationships between the major biomes of the Earth and the climatic factors of temperature and precipitation. The tundra biome is found only in regions of low temperature and low precipitation.*

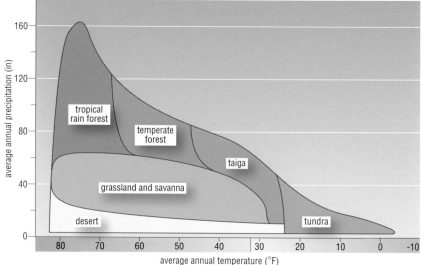

are therefore restricted to the upper left region of the diagram. Grasslands occur over a wide range of temperature, depending on whether they are tropical savannas or temperate prairies, but need less rainfall than forests, so they lie below these on the graph. Deserts can also occur in hot or cold regions of the world, but characteristically they occupy very dry climatic regions, so they lie at the base of the graph. Tundra is found in the bottom right-hand corner. Its climate is both cold and dry.

Climate is clearly the key to tundra distribution, therefore, and in order to understand the pattern of tundra over the surface of the Earth it is necessary to consider what controls the world's climate patterns.

## The Earth's climate patterns

The Earth receives most of its heat from sunlight that strikes the land surface, warming it. The ocean surfaces are also warmed in this way, but much of the energy that falls upon them is reflected, so that the warming effect is generally less than on land surfaces (see the sidebar "Albedo," page 15). The high latitudes (that is, the regions most distant from the equator) receive less energy from the Sun than do the low (tropical) latitudes. There are two main reasons why this is the case. The first is related to the angle at which the Sun's rays strike the Earth, as shown in the illustration on page 8. At the equator, the Sun is almost directly overhead for much of the year, while in the high latitudes the same amount of solar energy is spread over almost twice the land surface area because of the low angle that is achieved. The second factor that has to be considered is the thickness of atmosphere that the Sun's rays have to pass through to arrive at the Earth's surface. When the light comes vertically through the atmosphere (as at times in the Tropics), it passes through less atmosphere than in the polar regions. The atmosphere dissipates some light energy, especially if there is dust or impurity present, so less energy reaches the ground. This again means that the polar regions are starved of energy in relation to the Tropics. Exactly how much energy is lost in this way depends upon numerous factors, such as cloud cover, high-altitude

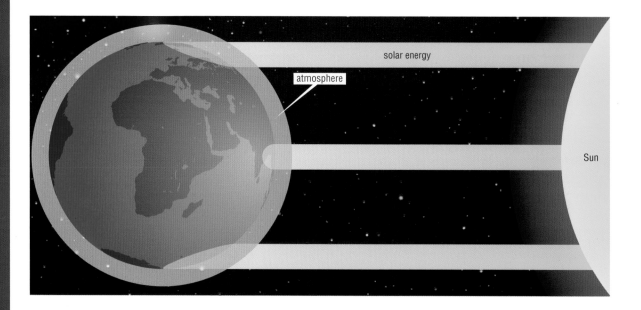

solar energy

atmosphere

Sun

*Incident solar energy on the surface of the Earth during a Northern Hemisphere summer. Energy is spread over a greater area near the North and South Poles than at the equator. The sunlight also passes through a greater thickness of atmosphere at the poles, so more energy is absorbed or reflected.*

dust caused by volcanic eruptions, and the precise angle at which the sunlight strikes the atmosphere. In general, however, the equatorial regions receive about six times the amount of incident energy from the Sun per unit area when compared with the polar regions.

At the same time as energy is arriving at the surface of the Earth, it is also being radiated from the Earth back into space, but the overall balance varies from one part of the planet to another. In the low latitudes, more energy is arriving than is leaving, creating an energy surplus that becomes dispersed by movements of the atmosphere and the ocean currents. But in the high latitudes, especially those between 75°N or 75°S and the poles, more energy is being radiated than is received. So these polar regions are in an energy deficit. If there were no mechanisms by which energy was redistributed around the world, then one would expect the equatorial regions to be 25°F (14°C) warmer than they actually are, and the poles would be 45°F (25°C) colder. As it is, the atmosphere and the oceans are moderating the temperature differences between equator and poles.

Seasonal changes also contribute to the uneven distribution of energy over the surface of the Earth. Seasonal variations in climate result from the fact that the Earth is tilted, not upright, on its axis. This angle varies and is currently 23.5 degrees. The Earth orbits the Sun once a year and the effect of the tilt is to create the different seasons (see illustration below). When the tilt of the Earth brings the North Pole toward the Sun, the Northern Hemisphere experiences summer conditions. Conversely, when the South Pole is pointed toward the Sun, the Northern Hemisphere is in winter. In the Tropics, between 23.5°N and 23.5°S, the Sun is directly overhead twice a year and is always high in the sky at noon. But in the high latitudes, the seasonal variation is more severe. Regions at latitudes higher than 66.5°N or 66.5°S of the equator (that is, 90 minus 23.5) will experience certain days in the winter when the Sun does not rise above the horizon. In the north of Ellesmere Island in northern Canada, for example, the Sun rises above the horizon for only 143 days of the year. For the remaining 222 days of the year the area is in darkness or dim twilight. Conversely, during the summer period, there are nights within these polar realms when the Sun never sets. The latitudes of 66.5° therefore mark important limits around the poles and are called the Arctic and Antarctic Circles, respectively.

The uneven heating of the Earth's surface creates turbulence in the atmosphere. Light energy striking the land sur-

*The tilt of the Earth on its axis results in seasonal variation in climate. In the Northern Hemisphere, days are longer when the axis tilts toward the Sun (summer) and shorter when the tilt is away from the Sun (winter).*

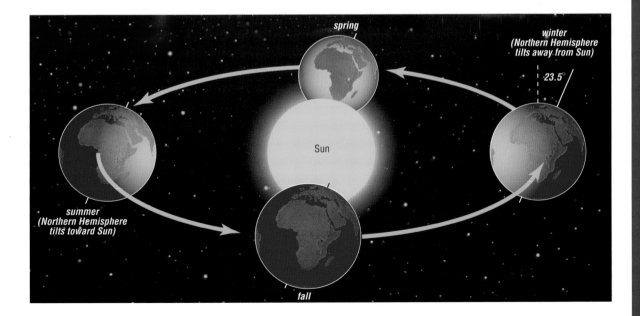

spring

winter
(Northern Hemisphere
tilts away from Sun)

23.5°

Sun

summer
(Northern Hemisphere
tilts toward Sun)

fall

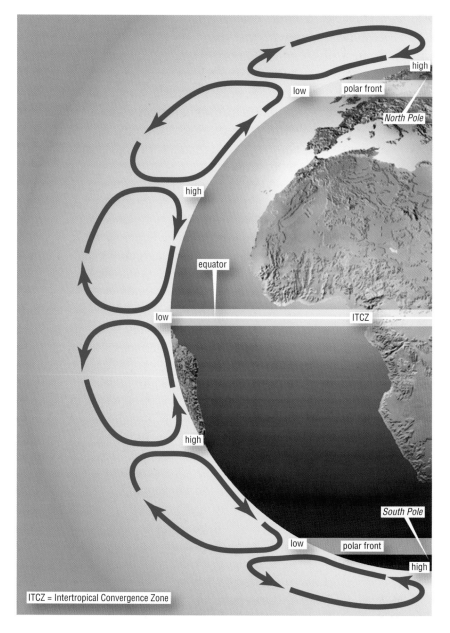

*The circulation cells of the atmosphere redistribute energy around the Earth. Descending air produces high-pressure areas in the subtropics and in the polar regions, while rising air results in low pressure close to the equator and around the polar front.*

face is converted to heat, and the air in contact with the heated land becomes warmed. Warm air is less dense than cold air, so it is forced upward from the hot equatorial regions by cooler, denser air that moves toward the equator from higher latitudes (see illustration above). This convergence of air masses forcing up the heated air over the equator is called the Intertropical Convergence Zone (ITCZ). Hot air is capable of holding more water vapor than is cold air and the rising air over the equator is heavily laden with water. But as it is forced upward it cools and the water vapor condenses into clouds and rain, so the equatorial region has a wet, rainy climate. The constant upward movement of air means that low atmospheric pressure predominates in the region. As more and more air rises over the equator, these cooling air masses are forced north and south, but because they are now colder they are also denser and begin to fall. The descent of the dense air takes place in the regions of 25° to 30° latitude north and south of the equator and results in the development of two belts of high atmospheric pressure around the world. As it descends, the air comes into contact with land surfaces once more, becomes heated by them, and takes up moisture from the environment. The outcome is that the high-pressure belts are arid and are the location of the world's great deserts.

Some of the descending air moves back toward the equator and the Intertropical Convergence Zone, but some heads toward the poles, taking some of the low-latitude heat energy into the higher latitudes and assisting in the redistribution of energy over the planet. When these poleward-moving masses of air reach latitudes of 50° to 60° north and south of the equator, they meet cold, dense polar air heading toward the equator, and the warmer, lighter air masses are forced upward, creating a low-pressure zone. This low-pressure zone is called the polar front. Once again, the upward movement of warm, moist air creates wet, climatically unstable conditions. Some of the air pushed upward in this low-pressure zone moves on to the poles, where it descends once more, creating patches of high pressure with low precipitation at the North and South Poles. Climatically, the polar regions are cold deserts. The movement of air masses over the surface of the Earth is further complicated by the spin of the planet on its axis. The Earth is spinning from west to east, so air moving toward the equator (including the cold polar air) is deflected to the west. This can affect the position of the polar front and set in motion swirling low-pressure systems called depressions that track from west to east over the temperate zone.

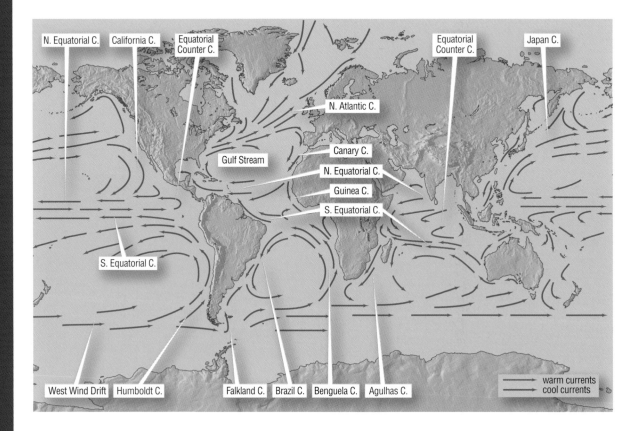

N. Equatorial C. | California C. | Equatorial Counter C. | Equatorial Counter C. | Japan C.

N. Atlantic C.

Canary C.

Gulf Stream

N. Equatorial C.

Guinea C.

S. Equatorial C.

S. Equatorial C.

West Wind Drift | Humboldt C. | Falkland C. | Brazil C. | Benguela C. | Agulhas C.

warm currents
cool currents

*Circulation patterns in the Earth's oceans. Note that the warm waters of the Gulf Stream penetrate into the Arctic Ocean from the North Atlantic, but there is no such warm movement in the North Pacific. As a result northern Alaska is much colder than northern Scandinavia. (See also the illustration on page 141.)*

Air masses thus assist in the dispersal of heat around the world, ensuring that the overall temperature difference between the equator and the poles is not as great as one would expect from studies of solar energy input. Ocean currents also have an important role in global heat transfers (see illustration above). In the eastern Atlantic, warm water from the Caribbean region, called the Gulf Stream, moves north and east, becoming the North Atlantic Drift, which warms the western coast of Europe. Bergen, in Norway, is at the same latitude as the southern tip of Greenland and of Baffin Island in Canada. But Bergen lies within the coniferous forest (or taiga) biome, well to the south of the tundra, while Greenland and Baffin Island lie deep in the tundra biome. Warmed by the ocean currents of the east Atlantic region, the climate of Bergen is warm enough to support forest growth. There is also a warm North Pacific Drift, but this does not penetrate past the Aleutian Islands because of the southward-moving cold waters from the Arctic. It is deflected southeast-ward toward Seattle and Vancouver, where it brings abundant precipitation to the temperate rain forests of the Pacific Northwest of North America.

The movement of warm water in the eastern Atlantic has a strong impact, therefore, on the distribution of tundra in northwestern Europe, pushing it northward by warming the climate of the region. In the western Atlantic Ocean, however, cold polar water also flows south from the Arctic Ocean between Greenland and eastern Canada, cooling these regions and encouraging a southward development of tundra. The North Pacific Ocean is also chilled by cold water currents from the Arctic Ocean moving southward through the narrow straits between Alaska and eastern Russia, chilling the Bering Sea and the Aleutian Islands.

Water loses its heat more slowly than landmasses do when conditions become cool, so all areas of land that are close to the sea are kept warmer as a result, even if there are no warm currents present. Continental landmasses gain and lose heat much more rapidly than the coastal regions, so that they become hotter in summer and cooler in winter. This can affect the distribution of vegetation. The boundary between the tundra and the forest in Alaska and the Yukon Territories, for example, lies at about 69°N, while in eastern Canada, in the Hudson Bay region, the boundary lies much farther from the pole, at close to 55°N. This is due in part to the very cold winters in the continental interior of eastern North America that hold back the northward extension of forest and favor the tundra. The same applies to eastern Russia; the coldest place on Earth is the north of Siberia.

When all of these different factors are considered, it becomes clear that the polar regions of the world are going to be cold. They receive less energy from the Sun, and the influence of warm currents and warm air masses from the equatorial regions is very limited. Where warm currents do penetrate, as in the eastern Atlantic Ocean, the climate is correspondingly warmer. The coldness of the landmasses is also lessened to a certain degree when the ocean lies close by; the coldest parts of the polar regions lie away from oceanic influence.

## Climate in the polar tundra

At the South Pole lies the great continent of Antarctica, which is covered by the world's largest ice sheet. The influence of the oceans is felt only along its fringes, so the interior is incapable of supporting tundra vegetation. Almost the entire continent lies within the Antarctic Circle, the exception being the Antarctic Peninsula, which extends north toward the tip of South America. Most of the landmass, in fact, lies within the latitude 70°S. Surrounded by oceans and confined within these high latitudes, these lands display no transition of vegetation from the polar ice to temperate forests, as is the case in the Northern Hemisphere. The tundra of the Antarctic is therefore isolated on the coastal fringe of the continent, the Antarctic Peninsula, and some islands of the Southern Ocean.

In the Northern Hemisphere there is no ice sheet over the North Pole because it lies within the Arctic Ocean. The lands fringing that ocean and the North Atlantic and North Pacific regions bear tundra vegetation, and at its southern edge this tundra is bounded by the boreal forests of birch, pine, spruce, and larch. This border forms a timberline, beyond which the growth of tall trees is severely limited and only shrub growth is possible. This timberline corresponds quite closely with the average July temperature of 50°F (10°C). A line joining all the places that share a particular temperature is called an isotherm, and this average 50°F July isotherm correlates well with the timberline. In other words, if the average temperature in July is less than this value, healthy tree growth becomes very difficult. This summer temperature factor, therefore, seems to be the maximum tolerated by the tundra biome.

Low temperature within the tundra biome is partly determined by the nature of the ground cover. One inevitable feature of the tundra landscape, as a consequence of its generally low temperature, is the presence of areas of snow and ice. The occurrence of water in these solid forms results in the loss of further energy, because the sunlight is reflected off their white surfaces and is not absorbed by the ground beneath. The degree to which a material reflects light is termed its *albedo* (see sidebar on opposite page).

Snow and ice, therefore, have a high albedo, meaning that they reflect much of the light that reaches their surfaces, while dark rocks, organic soils, and many types of vegetation cover

## Albedo

*Albedo* can be defined as the proportion of incoming solar radiation that is reflected from a surface. Pale, shiny surfaces reflect much of the light that is incident upon them, while dark, dull surfaces absorb most of the incoming energy. The albedo value is usually expressed as a decimal, so that an albedo of 0.9 means that 90 percent of the incoming radiation is reflected, while an albedo of 0.1 means that only 10 percent is reflected. The reflected energy is measured either by an instrument located a few feet above the surface or, on a larger scale, it can be measured from a low-flying aircraft. The following table gives some albedo values for different kinds of surfaces.

| | |
|---|---|
| Fresh snow | 0.75–0.95 |
| Old snow | 0.45–0.70 |
| Snow-covered vegetation | 0.25–0.80 |
| Open tundra | 0.15–0.20 |
| Coniferous forest | 0.05–0.15 |

generally have a lower albedo. The heat absorption by the darker areas and objects in a tundra landscape can create differences in the local climate, but the generally white surface of the tundra helps to keep the region cold. This can operate even on a very small scale in a microclimate rather than a climate. The soil surface absorbs sunlight and becomes warmer, often by 1°F (0.5°C), than the air temperature above. Even small differences can be critical for living plants and other organisms. Dark stones in the ground can act as heat absorbers, and thin layers of gradually melting ice can behave like miniature greenhouses, raising the local temperature near the soil.

Taking into account the average temperature through the entire year, tundra habitats are limited to regions with an average below about 25°F (–4°C). But average temperatures do not give a full impression of the climate of an area. The temperature on a single day in July, usually the warmest month of summer, can rise as high as 86°F (30°C), especially in continental sites, such as eastern Canada or Siberia. But the nighttime temperatures are low, so the average for the month remains below 50°F (10°C). The length of the summer season is also important for tundra plants and animals because they have to complete their reproductive cycles in a limited period. In Churchill, Manitoba, for example, only during the months of June, July, August, and September does the mean temperature rise above freezing (see graph below). At Isachsen, in the Northwest Territories of Canada, however, July may be the only month in the year with an average temperature above freezing. This places a much greater strain on the organisms inhabiting the region. Both of these sites are examples of polar tundra, and in the graph their climates are contrasted with that of alpine tundra at Niwot Ridge, Colorado (see "Climate in the alpine tundra," pages 18–22).

The overall climate of the Arctic tundra thus consists of long, extremely cold winters and short, cool summers. The seasonal range of temperature is considerable, mainly as a result of the absence of solar energy input in winter. The diurnal (daily) range of temperature, however, tends to be relatively small as a consequence of the low Sun angle and the constant night in winter and day in summer. The Antarctic, which has extensive ice sheets and high mountains, is generally colder than the Arctic, which is one reason why it is so poor in flowering plant life.

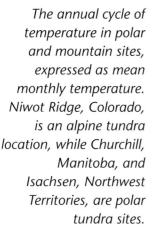

*The annual cycle of temperature in polar and mountain sites, expressed as mean monthly temperature. Niwot Ridge, Colorado, is an alpine tundra location, while Churchill, Manitoba, and Isachsen, Northwest Territories, are polar tundra sites.*

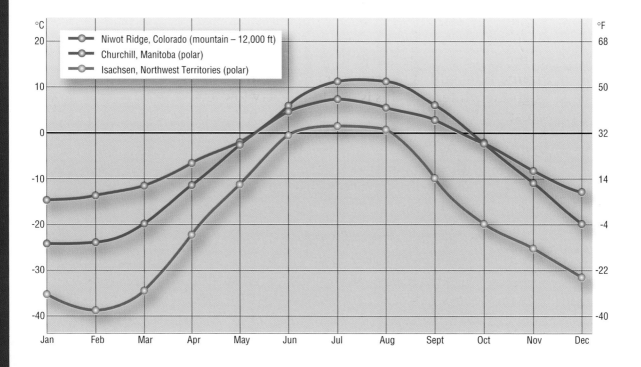

The polar tundra of the Northern Hemisphere is found in a zone where climate varies very considerably, from the forest in the south to the ice in the north. Geographers have found it convenient to divide this into two distinct zones, the Low Arctic and the High Arctic. The term *High Arctic* is usually used for the most northerly groups of islands between the North Pole and Canada, Russia, Scandinavia, and Greenland, lying north of latitude 75°N. The term *Low Arctic,* on the other hand, is generally used for the more southerly mainland areas of tundra. The growing season in the Low Arctic can be between three and five months, but in the High Arctic it is generally less than two and a half months. In the Low Arctic, the mean July temperature is around 46°F to 50°F (8°C to 10°C) and in the High Arctic is only 38°F to 43°F (3°C to 6°C). The vegetation of these two regions varies significantly as a consequence of the climatic differences, as will be seen later (see "Arctic tundra vegetation," pages 23–26).

The climate of the tundra is not only cold, it is also dry, especially in the polar regions. The annual total precipitation (including rain and snow) in polar tundra does not normally exceed 10 inches (25 cm). For this reason, the tundra regions are often referred to as "cold deserts." Although the low temperature is generally very obvious to any visitor to the tundra, the dryness of the climate might not be so apparent. The ground is mainly wet in summer and rich in ice and snow through the winter, but this is due to the very low levels of evaporation. What precipitation falls generally fails to evaporate back into the atmosphere; it either freezes, remains in pools, or moves over the surface in streams and rivers. The polar regions of the High Arctic have even less precipitation than the surrounding ring of Low Arctic tundra. True polar desert usually receives less than 4.3 inches (11 cm) of precipitation (usually snow) in a year. This is comparable to the rainfall in a low-latitude hot desert. For instance, Death Valley in California generally receives 1.5 inches (4 cm) of rainfall a year and the average for the Mojave Desert is nearer to eight inches (20 cm). So the polar regions really can be very dry, and the use of the term *polar desert* is entirely appropriate.

## Climate in the alpine tundra

The climate of alpine tundra is more complicated than that of the polar tundra because so many factors affect the timberline and therefore the altitude at which tundra vegetation begins. Altitude itself is the dominant feature because the temperature of the atmosphere generally decreases as one goes higher. The rate at which temperature drops with altitude is called the *lapse rate* and this varies with a range of atmospheric conditions and geographical locations (see sidebar on opposite page).

Mountains in the high latitudes (closer to the poles) will bear tundra habitats at lower altitudes than mountains in the Tropics, because the temperature at the bottom of the mountain will be lower to start with. Even in a single range of mountains, it is found that the timberline is higher as one approaches the equator. In the Sierra Nevada of California, for example, the timberline is around 1,000 feet (300 m) higher at the southern end than at the northern end around 300 miles (500 km) away. For every one degree of latitude closer to the equator, the timberline rises by about 360 feet (110 m). Mountains in the Tropics, therefore, need to be very high in order to support tundra (or, to put it another way, to fail to support forest). The illustration on page 20 shows the relative heights and latitudes of some major mountain ranges and indicates the altitudes at which the timberlines are to be found. There is a marked increase in the altitude of the timberline from higher latitudes (closer to the poles) to lower latitudes (closer to the equator).

The average annual temperature in alpine tundra locations is similar to that of the polar tundra sites. Detailed climate records are available from many mountain sites, such as Niwot Ridge in Colorado (see the graph on page 16). Here, the mean July temperature is 46°F (8°C) at an altitude of 12,300 feet (3,750 m), but the average in December and January is only 9°F (–13°C). The seasonal variation in temperature, therefore, is less extreme than that of an Arctic site, such as Churchill, Manitoba, as shown in the diagram. In alpine tundra habitats, this seasonal variation in temperature depends upon latitude. High-latitude mountains, close to or within the Arctic Circle, have the same wide range of seasonal variation as the Arctic tundra, but sites closer to the equator, such as the

## Lapse rate

When a fixed amount of air (for convenience called a "package") is in contact with a hot land surface, it absorbs heat and it expands. This means that the molecules within the package of air occupy more space and the air becomes less dense. When air is less dense than the air above it, it rises, being displaced by the denser air. As it rises, the package of warm air is subject to less and less atmospheric pressure because it has less weight of air pressing down upon it from above, and the lower pressure means that it expands. The molecules in expanding gas have to push other molecules out of their way, and doing so slows down their movements and causes them to lose energy; in other words, the gas cools. This is called *adiabatic cooling;* the word *adiabatic* means that there is no energy exchange between the gas and its surroundings. Adiabatic cooling resulting from gas expansion with altitude causes a general decline (or lapse) in air temperature with height above the ground, and the rate at which this occurs is called the dry adiabatic lapse rate.

The adiabatic cooling of the air, however, means that it cannot hold as much water vapor, because warm air has a higher capacity for water-holding than cold air. As the air in the package cools, therefore, its water vapor condenses into droplets. A special property of water comes into play here: its resistance to changes of physical state. Water occurs in three physical states—solid (ice), liquid, and gas (water vapor)—and a change of state requires a relatively large gain or loss of energy. When water changes state it either absorbs or releases energy in the form of heat, called *latent heat*. During condensation water releases some of this energy, warming the air. The actual observed lapse rate at any location results from a combination of the two processes of dry adiabatic cooling and the additional input of latent heat. This will vary depending on such factors as the humidity of the atmosphere, but a general figure is approximately 3.6°F fall in temperature for every gain of 1,000 feet in altitude (6.5°C fall for every 1,000 m).

high Ruwenzori Mountains of Uganda or Mount Kilimanjaro in Kenya, have little variation in their overall climate through the year. In alpine tundra, however, the daily variation in temperature is often extreme. On Mount Kenya in East Africa, for example, at 13,800 feet (4,200 m) the air temperature may rise to 60°F (15°C) in the day and fall to 23°F (–5°C) in the night, and this can present considerable problems to the plants inhabiting such a location. This degree variation between night and day temperatures is not found in the polar tundra, where the Sun hardly sets in the summer and

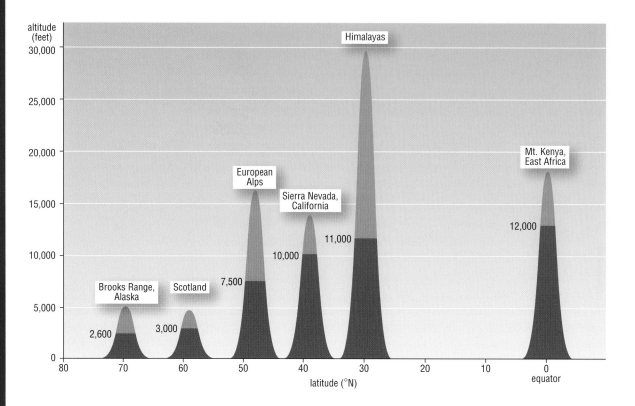

*A selection of Northern Hemisphere mountains bearing alpine tundra. The closer a mountain is to the equator, the higher the altitude at which the tundra biome is found.*

hardly rises during the polar winter. The range of temperature between day and night is thus relatively small.

An additional climatic factor of importance in both alpine and polar tundra is wind action. High wind speeds remove the layer of air close to the ground, which is often the warmest air when vegetation is present because of the heat absorption by dark surfaces. If this warm layer is stripped away it leaves vegetation and soil cold. The presence of ice crystals in the wind adds to its abrasive capacity and is particularly harmful to plants that emerge. For this reason, wind is an important factor in determining the altitude of the timberline on mountains. The direction of the prevailing winds can often be detected from the pattern of the forest/tundra border on mountains. In the Sierra Nevada of California, for example, tundra vegetation can be found at lower elevations on the western side of the mountains (facing the Pacific Ocean) than on the east. On the west, the limit of subalpine forest is about 10,500 feet (3,200 m), while on the protected eastern side it is at about 11,800 feet (3,600 m). High winds may completely eliminate trees and produce a more tundra-like vegetation in lower latitudes than one would expect on the basis of temperature, especially in oceanic regions (that is, areas close to the oceans and strongly influenced by them). Such oceanic, tundralike vegetation is found in Newfoundland and northern Scotland, both in the North Atlantic, and in Tierra del Fuego in South America. The microclimate of mountains is made even more complicated by the varied topography. The steepness and the aspect (the direction a slope is facing, north or south) influence how much sunlight reaches any particular location, so forest can extend to higher altitude on south-facing slopes. As a result, timberlines are often ragged and do not run neatly along the contours of mountains. It is the height of the timberline that determines how low down a mountain alpine tundra is able to develop.

Arctic tundra, as has been described, is effectively a cold desert. The descending air masses at the poles bring little precipitation (see the illustration on page 10). In mountain sites, on the other hand, air from lowland regions or from the oceans is often pushed by winds and forced upward over the mountain ranges. As air cools, its water-holding capacity is reduced and its water content condenses as cloud; this may then precipitate as rain droplets or, if the temperature is sufficiently low, snow. The side of the mountain facing the prevailing winds is subject to the highest levels of precipitation. In the sheltered lee of the mountain, air descends once again and precipitation is less intense. The lee side of the mountain is said to lie in a rain-shadow, producing drier conditions.

In general, precipitation increases with altitude. In the Rocky Mountains, to the west of Boulder, Colorado, for example, at an altitude of 5,250 feet (1,603 m) the average annual temperature is 48°F (8.8°C) and the annual precipitation is 15.5 inches (395 mm). At altitude 8,460 feet (2,580 m) temperature is 42°F (5.6°C) and precipitation 21.3 inches (540 mm), while at altitude 12,300 feet (3,750 m), temperature is 26°F (–3.3°C) and precipitation 25.2 inches (641 mm). By comparison, the data for Fort Yukon, Alaska, at an altitude of 416 feet (127 m), show an average annual temperature of 20°F (–6.7°C) and an annual precipitation of 6.8 inches (172 mm).

One final factor of the physical environment of alpine habitats that needs to be considered is the low air pressure and consequently the low availability of oxygen. This is especially important to active animals, which need oxygen for their respiration. The oxygen density at 18,000 feet (5,500 m) is only half that found at sea level, so animals, including human climbers, find strenuous activity particularly difficult there. Most mammals, even wild sheep and ibex, are largely limited to altitudes below 19,000 feet (5,800 m). Birds and some cold-blooded invertebrate animals, however, are able to exist even higher (see "Tundra invertebrates," pages 98–102, and "Tundra birds," pages 102–111).

## Diversity of tundra landscapes

The tundra is not a uniform biome; its general form, or landscape topography, is very variable. In the Arctic, high mountains are found in some regions, such as the Brooks Range of Alaska, which forms the southern limit of the tundra in that state. Between the mountains of the Brooks Range and the Arctic Ocean lies a plateau of foothills and then a strip of flat coastal plain. The plain gives a generally uniform impression of extensive flat lands but has numerous local landscape features, including lakes, bogs, and patterned lands. Much of the tundra of northern Canada is also relatively flat and it is crossed by some major rivers, such as the Mackenzie River. The landscape becomes more mountainous again in the east, where the Torngat Mountains of Labrador rise to more than 6,500 feet (2,000 m). Scattered along the north Canadian coastline are many islands, including some of the largest islands in the world, such as Baffin Island. Farther east lies the massive island of Greenland, whose interior (80 percent of the total area) is covered by a permanent ice sheet. Along its eastern coast are high mountains, through which the ice spills as a series of mountain glaciers. Out in the North Atlantic lie the islands of Jan Mayen and Svalbard. Svalbard consists of a group of five major islands and has rugged mountain topography and a coastline of deep fjords. The remainder of the Arctic tundra lies within northern Scandinavia and Russia. Much of this vast area consists of an extensive flat plain, split from north to south by the Ural Mountains, which continue northward in the form of the islands of Novaya Zemlya. To the west of this divide lies the Russian Plain, and to the east is the Siberian Plain. These flat lands have much in common with the coastal plain of northern Alaska. Despite this great variety in landscape, all these habitats are components of the tundra biome and all support tundra vegetation.

In the Antarctic, the world's largest ice sheet covers most of the continent, so the landscape is essentially ice-dominated apart from some projecting mountain peaks. Beneath the ice lies a landscape that is only just being discovered as techniques of coring and mapping improve. One newly discovered feature is the existence of lakes of great antiquity beneath the ice, and these will undoubtedly prove of interest to geologists, chemists, and microbiologists. The abundance of ice, the very cold climate, and the lack of exposed land surface means that true tundra vegetation is scarce and mainly coastal. Patches of lichen and moss, together with small quantities of grass, are able to survive in the limited patches of land that are free of snow and ice.

As discussed previously, the climate of the polar tundra changes as one approaches the poles, and the nature of the landscape and vegetation reflects this. It is possible to divide these tundra regions into different zones. One must remember, however, that strict lines of division cannot usually be discerned; the landscape gradually changes with increasing latitude. In the Southern Hemisphere, the isolation of the Antarctic continent by oceans disrupts any zonation, so there is no transition between tundra and forest as in the Arctic regions.

## Arctic tundra vegetation

In the Arctic, at the northern edge of the forest, where tree growth becomes difficult because of the short summer season and the intense cold and wind blasting, is a zone called *forest tundra*. This represents the southern limit of the Low Arctic, and the trees here are scattered and stunted. In North America, black spruce and tamarack (on wetter areas) and white spruce (on drier soils) often form the timberline. But nonconiferous trees can also form an abundant component of the flora, including balsam poplar, paper birch, and alder. Pines are

*Shrub tundra in the Low Arctic. An autumn landscape in Denali National Park, Alaska (Photo by Michio Hoshino)*

rarely found in the Arctic timberline of Alaska or Canada, but they are widespread in Europe and Asia, particularly the Scots pine (*Pinus sylvestris*). Isolated trees, sometimes contorted into twisted shapes by the wind, may grow on favorable sites, or sometimes groups of trees survive in sheltered hollows, protected from the wind. Beneath the trees is a dense layer of shrubs and herbs. This zone is really a transition between the boreal forest or taiga (the biome that forms a zone in the latitudes below the tundra) and the true tundra. Ecologists refer to such gradual boundaries as *ecotones*.

Beyond the zone of true tree growth, in the Low Arctic, the rolling landscape is dominated by low woody plants, forming the *tall shrub tundra*. The shrubs are characteristically less than three feet (1 m) in height but may occasionally grow as high as six feet (2 m). Some dwarf trees and shrubs are contained within this vegetation, largely dwarf birches and willows, together with alder. Among these are other shrubs, mainly evergreens, including Labrador tea and several species of cranberry and crowberry.

In more exposed sites and in the more northern regions of the Low Arctic, *dwarf shrub tundra* becomes the dominant vegetation type. The taller species are no longer present and the general vegetation canopy is only around one to two feet (20 to 40 cm) above the ground surface. The main components are still woody plants forming a dense thicket, and these include bearberry and crowberry, together with cotton grasses. In some places the cotton grasses may assume dominance and the landscape becomes what may be termed *tussock-heath tundra*. This type of tundra is particularly well developed in Alaska, western Canada, and eastern Siberia.

The main difference between the High Arctic and the Low Arctic is that the vegetation in the High Arctic is composed largely of herbaceous plants rather than woody ones. This is called *grass-moss tundra*. Here, the intensity of cold, the very short growing season, and the constant blasting of winds that often carry ice crystals make growth very difficult for any plant that extends far above ground level, so the characteristic growth form is a cushion clinging closely to the soil surface. The wind trims the tops of these cushions and prevents them from growing higher, especially over the tops of exposed ridges, where summer drought may also constrain growth. Just how long the summer growing season lasts is dependent in part on the local topography, because the sheltered hollows often have patches of snow that last well into the early summer, and this restricts the time for growth and reproduction. Areas of late-remaining snow are usually dominated by mosses rather than the grasses, sedges, or other flowering plants.

Melting snow creates an abundance of water in the summer. At the same time, the rates of evaporation are low, so most low-lying areas become wetlands despite the low rainfall. The action of frost often creates complicated patterns on the ground surface, with ridges and hollows (see "Patterns on the ground," pages 46–53), and the hollows develop into pools with sedge-dominated edges. These wet tundra habitats of the High Arctic become valuable breeding areas for wading birds and other wildfowl during the summer.

Away from the wetland sites, however, the High Arctic drought has a strong impact upon the vegetation and the landscape. Scattered grasses, mosses, and cushion plants form an open vegetation known as the *High Arctic semidesert.* Lichens and mosses often account for half of the vegetation cover, and a range of drought-resistant tundra plants joins the community, including saxifrages and mountain avens. Farther north, more of the soil becomes visible as the vegetation thins. This is the true polar desert in which only scattered plants grow. It eventually meets the Arctic Ocean or the permanent ice.

## Alpine tundra vegetation

Alpine tundra contains a range of vegetation zones very similar to those of the Arctic, but they are arranged in relation to altitude rather than latitude. The environment again stretches from the timberline at its lower end to the bare mountain peak or the ice of a glacier. Mountain timberlines, rather like the Arctic timberlines, are often a ragged affair of stunted and twisted individual trees that somehow manage to survive after a chance germination in this harsh terrain. In sheltered valleys, the trees may extend a little higher than in the more exposed locations, and there is sometimes an ecotone of dwarf trees around the limits of their growth. German botanists coined a very expressive word for this stunted tree zone, calling it *krummholz,* literally "crooked wood." The zone is present, however, only where the natural transition between forest and alpine tundra vegetation has developed. Often people have interfered with this boundary, especially in the more heavily populated mountainous regions of the world, where the high tundra and grasslands have been used for sheep and cattle grazing. In many mountain regions, domestic animals have been taken to the high regions each summer, grazing not only on the grasses and herbs but also on the young trees. This additional stress has usually eliminated the krummholz zone and in places even lowered the timberline, creating a grassland/tundra transition zone.

There are some locations where the altitudinal limit to tree growth may be determined not by climate nor by human activity but by soil factors. In the southern Appalachian Mountains and in Montana, grassy "balds" occur on the summits of some mountains. These areas have shallow soils and are exposed to intense drought in summer, so tree invasion is not possible and instead a kind of grass subalpine vegetation develops. Generally, however, it is the cold climate that limits the forest and leaves the habitat open to alpine tundra vegetation. Timberlines are often lower on the northern aspect of mountains, where the sunshine does not penetrate well. In the Brooks Range of southern Alaska, for example, woodland may extend to around 3,000 feet (1,000 m) on the south-facing slopes while attaining only 2,000 feet (700 m) on the northern side.

High mountains in the Tropics, such as Mount Kenya in East Africa, display a series of vegetation zones at different heights. The illustration on page 28 shows this zonation with altitude. The mountain, which is situated close to the equator, has tropical savanna and forest at its base. At higher altitudes these types of tropical vegetation give way to a more temperate forest of bamboo, which is succeeded by a shrub zone of heath plants. Above 12,000 feet (3,600 m) the alpine tundra biome is found, and above this altitude lies the permanent snow.

As in the case of the Arctic tundra, it is possible to recognize different vegetation types in the alpine tundra. Shrub tundra is found in the lower and less exposed regions, as seen on Mount Kenya, and contains several of the plants of the heath family (Ericaceae). Some of these are also found in the Arctic, including crowberry and bearberry. Grass and cushion-plant tundra is present in the more exposed, colder, and drier sites, and this thins out to lichen and moss vegetation as soils become thin and rock debris is the main constituent of the soil. Within the alpine landscape, it is also possible to distinguish wet meadows, dry meadows, and bare rocky regions with limited vegetation cover, called *fellfields*. These vegetation types reflect the increasing degree of drought resulting from topographic position (hollows and ridges) and the relative depth and drainage in the soil.

In both the Arctic and the alpine tundra landscapes, snow plays an important part. Snowflakes are formed in the air when the temperature falls below freezing and water droplets become crystallized before settling. On the ground, they begin to lose their crystal form over a few days, sometimes melting and refreezing to form a more powdery or granular

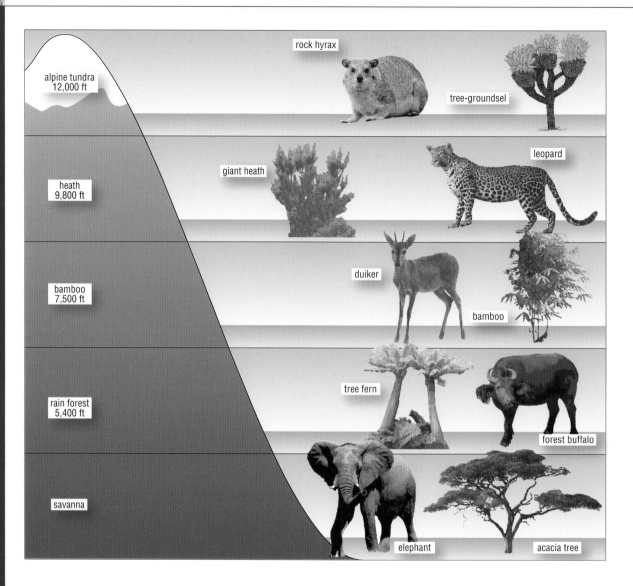

*The major zones of vegetation found at different altitudes on Mount Kenya in East Africa. This tropical mountain lies on the equator yet has tundra vegetation near its summit.*

material over the course of years. This is called *firn.* As new snow accumulates from above, firn becomes compressed and compacted into ice, and in this way, over the course of about 10 years, the snow becomes fully incorporated into an ice mass, or glacier. But not all snow is converted to glacial ice; some simply melts with the coming of summer and exposes once again the land that it buried.

"Snow patches" are temporary accumulations of snow that may survive over a few years but never form true glaciers. Some melt each year and leave behind a wet patch of landscape, often in a sheltered hollow where the wind is not too corrosive and the Sun has limited powers of penetration. The snow has a number of effects upon the local climatic conditions. Its presence late into the spring means that the ground is protected from sunlight for longer; in other words, the snow patch effectively prolongs winter for the inhabitants of the soil it covers. But the snow also serves as a protective thermal blanket from the worst of the winter cold, so soils beneath the snow blanket remain warmer than those where snow is blown away and the frost can penetrate. Both plants and animals are affected by these two influences of a snow patch, and these habitats support different flora and fauna as a consequence. It is the property of thermal insulation in compacted snow, of course, that forms the basis for its use in the construction of an igloo. Here human beings are taking advantage of the very effective insulation that snow provides, for they can heat the inside of the igloo and raise the temperature below the snow blocks considerably above the outside air temperature, and the snow retains the hotter air. Many animals also use the snow in a similar way, burrowing within it to keep warm.

The general persistence of snow varies in different regions and in different microsites. Many tundra regions, such as the Siberian tundra, are covered by snow for 200 to 280 days in the year (compared with about 60 to 80 days in the Russian steppes, for instance). Its depth is also variable, but the tundra regions have low precipitation, so a snow depth of around eight to 12 inches (20 to 30 cm) is fairly typical. In alpine sites, on the other hand, precipitation can be high, so snow patches can be deep. The local topography, including slope, often limits the snow depth, and where deep snow can accumulate and persist, glaciers begin to form. Local landform can also be important in the tundra plains, because the wind will sweep snow from exposed ridges and raised areas and allow it to collect in hollows.

## Conclusions

Tundra is found in those parts of the Earth where conditions are extremely cold in their average temperature but are still able to support life. The high latitudes bear tundra because the amount of energy reaching these regions from the Sun is much lower than is found in the equatorial regions. The tilt of the Earth on its axis also produces great variations in seasonal conditions with extremely long days in the summer and very short days in winter.

The poles are regions of descending air masses, so they receive low precipitation. The South Pole occurs on a great landmass, Antarctica, and lies on the world's greatest ice sheet. The North Pole, on the other hand, occurs in the Arctic Ocean, so although there is pack ice, there is no ice sheet present. The landmass of Greenland does support an ice sheet. Antarctica is surrounded by oceans, so ice-free land is very limited and there is little tundra vegetation, but the Arctic Ocean is surrounded by the continents of North America and Eurasia, so much land is available for tundra vegetation, which grades southward into the boreal forest biome.

Alpine tundra is found scattered around the world wherever there are high mountains. Air temperature falls with altitude, so if the mountain is high enough, tundra ecosystems can develop even on tropical mountains. In the low latitudes, the seasonal differences in temperature are less than those found in the polar regions, but the differences between day and night are often greater. Precipitation is generally higher in the alpine tundra than in the polar tundra.

Tundra vegetation is similar in its basic structure in both polar and alpine habitats. Tall trees are absent, but stunted dwarf tree and shrub species can survive, generally extending less than two or three feet (1 m) above the ground. Grasses, sedges, mosses, and lichens cover the open patches of the ground. This vegetation is capable of withstanding cold, abrasive winds and periodic burial by snow. In the southern parts of the Arctic tundra, and at the lower boundary of alpine tundra, this vegetation type grades into stunted trees of birch, pine, spruce, and larch.

Tundra thus occupies the cold extremity of the Earth's varied climate. Its plants, animals, and microbes have been selected by nature to cope with the highly stressed conditions they must endure. The extremes of cold also have their impact on the rocks and the soils of the tundra region, as will be discussed in the next chapter.

# CHAPTER 2

# GEOLOGY OF THE TUNDRA

Geology is the study of rocks, their formation and their breakdown. Both processes are at work in the tundra regions. In the oceans adjacent to the tundra lands, and in the lakes that occupy some polar and alpine landscapes, eroded soils and rock fragments are constantly accumulating as sediments. These build up and eventually form the sedimentary rocks of the future. Volcanoes are active in some tundra regions, both polar and alpine, bringing from deep below the Earth's crust the molten rock that cools and hardens on the surface, forming new landscapes that will be invaded by tundra vegetation. Erosive forces are also active in the tundra, driven by low temperatures. Precipitation may accumulate as ice. The weight of ice upon the surface of the Earth's crust may depress it, and as it slides over the ground the mass of ice will grind down the rocks to the consistency of flour. This "rock flour" is then eroded by streams and rivers, which form from the melting ice and snow, and is redistributed over the landscape. Among the rock detritus left by the activity of ice, plants begin to grow and soils begin to form; the tundra ecosystem begins to evolve. The tundra regions are thus areas that are strongly affected by geological activity.

## Polar geology

As explained in chapter 1, most of the polar tundra habitats on Earth are found around the edge of the Arctic Ocean. The rocks of this region lie in three massive sections, called shields, which occupy the three continents that surround the Arctic Ocean. These are the Canadian Shield, which includes Greenland; the Fennoscandian Shield, covering northern Scandinavia and Finland in Europe; and the Angara Shield, extending through the northern edge of Asia.

The shield rocks are extremely ancient, having been formed in Precambrian times (more than 540 million years ago), when some of the world's oldest rocks were produced. The Earth is believed to have formed about 4.6 billion years ago, and Greenland contains some of the oldest rocks yet recorded, with an age of 3.8 billion years. The Precambrian is sometimes called the Cryptozoic eon (*cryptozoic* means "hidden life"). At this time the only life on Earth was minute, so fossils are rare. The Cryptozoic eon includes the bulk of the Earth's history (the first 4 billion years) and is followed by the Phanerozoic eon, in which all visible forms of life evolved. The Cryptozoic is divided into three eras: the Priscoan or Hadean era (about 4.6 billion to 4 billion years ago), the Archaean era (about 4 billion to 2.5 billion years ago), and the Proterozoic era (about 2.5 billion to 500 million years ago). It was during the Archaean era that the rocks of the great shields were formed.

The Archaean era was a time of crustal development as the Earth cooled. Afterward, during the Proterozoic era, the Archaean rocks were altered by intense heating and pressure, forming a compacted rock called *gneiss* (pronounced "nice"). This is the rock that dominates the northern shields. Rocks that have been melted, crushed, and transformed by these processes are known as *metamorphic rocks*. It is likely that these rocks once formed great mountains that have eroded away over time, leaving a much more level landscape. The rocks are generally hard and contain little in the way of plant nutrients, so they give rise to acidic, nutrient-poor soils. But the fact that the rocks are being ground to a pulp by ice action (see "Effects of glaciation," pages 40–43) does mean that soils are frequently replenished.

Some parts of the Arctic have evidence of past volcanic activity, such as Jan Mayen Island and Greenland. Indeed, volcanic activity still takes place in the region, but mainly under the sea. The island of Surtsey appeared overnight off the coast of Iceland as a result of the eruption of an underwater volcano in 1963. Volcanic activity is associated with the Mid-Atlantic Ridge, a seafloor line of volcanoes running right up the Atlantic and extending into the Arctic Ocean.

The Antarctic continent is almost totally covered by the Antarctic Ice Sheet, so the solid geology is visible only where mountaintops protrude through the ice or in those coastal regions where ice does not form a complete blanket. The underlying geology of Antarctica consists of Precambrian rocks, similar to those of the Arctic shields, but a series of younger rocks are also present, particularly in West Antarctica. The continent of Antarctica was at one time joined with all the other major landmasses of the Earth in a single supercontinent, linking Africa, India, and Australia. Fossils in the rocks show that the climate in the past was very different from that of present-day Antarctica. In Permian times, about 290 million years ago, broad-leaved deciduous forests grew close to what is now the South Pole, so the Earth must have been much warmer. The wood of these ancient forests has growth rings, showing that there were strong seasonal differences in climate even though the overall conditions must have been warmer than at present. The discovery of fossils of these *Glossopteris* trees by early explorers demonstrated the continuity of vegetation between Antarctica and Australia, where these fossils are also found, and led geologists to believe that the continents were once part of a single landmass (see the sidebar "Plate tectonics," page 34).

A major ridge of mountains runs from the eastern edge of the Antarctic Ross Ice Shelf and arcs close to the South Pole before extending along the line of the Antarctic Peninsula, west of the Ronne Ice Shelf (see the map on page 3). These mountains, called the Transantarctic Mountains, contain sandstone rocks that bear fossils of fish from the Devonian period and of dinosaurs from the Jurassic period. It was during the Cretaceous period, around 140 million years ago, that the great continent broke up. By 40 million years ago the last land connections with South America and Australia had been lost, and Antarctica was on its own.

## Mountain geology

Tundra habitats are found not only in the polar regions but also upon many of the world's mountains, even in the low, equatorial latitudes (see the map on page 4). The mountain regions of the world are very varied in their geology and the mountains may be formed from a whole range of rocks, both

## Plate tectonics

The relatively cool surface of the Earth, called the *lithosphere* or crust, is floating upon a molten core. Within this fluid core, convection currents occur, in which hot, less dense materials rise and cool, while dense materials descend. These currents cause the surface crust to strain and shift. The crust is not a uniform layer, but is divided into a series of plates, and the study of these plates and their movements is called plate tectonics.

In some regions, two plates are being pushed apart because hot material from the mantle breaks through the crust, forming a zone of volcanic activity. The Mid-Atlantic Ridge is one such region. It is a north-to-south-running line where rising hot and relatively low-density molten rock from deep in the Earth rises to the surface, causing the crust to split and move away from the line, both to the east and the west. So the seafloor of the Atlantic is spreading very slowly, widening between two and four inches (5 to 10 cm) per year; America and Europe are gently drifting apart. The distance sailed by Columbus in 1492 was approximately 150 feet (50 m) shorter than he would have to sail today. Another case of crustal spreading caused the fragmentation of the landmass that once contained Antarctica.

Crustal movements not only take continents away from one another; they can also result in collisions. One such collision, of India with Asia, caused the line of contact to buckle, thrusting up the Himalaya Mountain chain. When plates collide, one may slide over the top of the other, forcing some of the crustal material down into the molten mantle, and the region where this occurs is called a *subduction zone.*

volcanic and sedimentary. The forms of their landscape and their vegetation are often closely related to the nature of their rocks, especially the way in which they become eroded and the forms that they develop. The formation of mountains depends upon the movements of the Earth's crust (see the sidebar above).

The Alps of Europe were created by pressure of the African plate moving north into the Eurasian plate, beginning at the same time as the Himalayan uplift, around 5 million years ago. Since then the Alps have been forced upward about 6,500 feet (2,000 m) and the Himalayas about 10,000 feet (3,000 m). The Sierra Nevada of California is a younger range than either the Alps or the Himalayas. It was created within the last 3 million years by the crushing and movement of adjacent plates on the western side of North America. Within that time the Sierra Nevada have risen about 6,500 feet (2,000 m), and the area is still active, with relatively frequent earthquakes. In 1872, near the town of Lone Pine, California, a strong earthquake created cliffs of more than 20 feet (6.5 m) in height, showing that uplift of the mountains is still taking place. All mountains begin to be leveled as soon as they are formed, however, so even the relatively young Sierra Nevada have much evidence of erosion. Just like the Precambrian rocks of the northern shields of Canada and Fennoscandia, they will one day be worn down by the action of climate. One of the most active agents of erosion, both in the Arctic and the alpine tundra, is ice.

## Ice accumulation

Ice accumulates where there is an abundant supply of snow and where the temperature is low enough to prevent the snowfall from melting completely away. Snow crystals, with their complex and intricate forms, become altered within a matter of days after they settle. They fragment into pieces, they may melt in the sun, or they may become compacted by the accumulation of further snow. They become denser and harder, forming sugarlike grains that are crushed together, eliminating the air spaces (although some bubbles of gas may be permanently trapped within them). If temperatures are low enough to permit their survival, snowflakes will have changed their form totally within two years, to produce what has been referred to as firn, or "old snow." Within another three or four years, the firn will become compacted to glacial ice.

Although ice caps and glaciers are composed mainly of ice, they also contain many impurities. The snow that accumulates may contain a range of airborne contaminants, from dust and pollen grains to human-made pollutants. Especially in geologically active regions such as Iceland, where active volcanoes are present, volcanic dusts consisting of fine glass particles called *tephra* may settle in layers over glaciers during periods of eruption. These tephra layers become buried as further ice accumulates, and their presence provides a means of dating particular horizons in the ice mass. Meteorologists, for example, may take borings through the ice to determine how fast ice has accumulated in the past, and the tephra helps in determining dates. The chemistry of the fine tephra dust is very distinctive, and it is possible to identify the source of the eruption by analyzing the particles trapped in ice. The chemistry may even differ during separate eruptions, so that specific eruptions of particular volcanoes in the past can be identified.

## Ice sheets, ice caps, and glaciers

There are several types of ice accumulation on Earth, including ice sheets and glaciers. Only two true ice sheets now exist, one occupying most of the continent of Antarctica, and the other covering much of Greenland. The Antarctic Ice Sheet occupies an area twice the size of Australia, bigger than the whole of Canada. About 85 percent of the world's freshwater is locked up in that one mass of ice, which in places achieves a depth of 2.5 miles (4 km). Below it is a land surface, much of which lies below the current sea level, especially in the west (see the map on page 3). This is so because the massive weight of the ice sheet actually presses the Earth's crust deeper into the fluid layer of mantle beneath as their combined mass achieves equilibrium. Along the eastern edge of Antarctica and along the Transantarctic Ridge, on the other hand, are ranges of mountains, some of which are high enough to project above the ice surface. These mountainous projections are given the name *nunataks,* derived from the Inuit language. In between the western and eastern sections of the Antarctic Ice Sheet is a fairly flat area of ice, the Ross Ice Shelf. This ice shelf floats on the surface of the sea, which forms a bay penetrating deep into the heart of Antarctica toward the South Pole, and its eastern edge is fringed with high mountains.

The Greenland Ice Sheet is considerably smaller than that of Antarctica, but it is still as big as Mexico. It contains about a further 8 percent of the world's freshwater. The center of Greenland is an enormous basin surrounded by high mountains, and the ice sheet fills the basin and flows through the mountains to the North Atlantic Ocean, where it breaks up

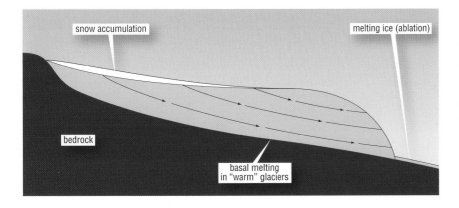

*Profile through the long axis of a valley glacier. Snow accumulates on the upper part of the glacier, where it is compressed into ice. In time the ice moves along the lines shown, eventually reaching the site of ice melt.*

into icebergs. In places this ice sheet reaches depths of about two miles (3 km). Scattered around the polar regions there are several smaller ice caps, often developed on high plateaus in mountainous regions. These are much smaller than the ice sheets but form centers of ice accumulation, from which the ice spreads outward in the form of glaciers. Such minor ice caps are found, for example, in Iceland and the Arctic island of Svalbard.

Glaciers are mobile masses of ice that radiate from ice sheets and ice caps or may form in the valleys of the mountain regions of the world. Glaciers are much smaller than ice sheets and ice caps, usually covering only a few square miles. Glaciers are common in the mountain regions of the far north and the far south, as in Alaska and New Zealand, but can also be found on high mountains nearer the equator, as in the Alps of Europe, the Himalayas of Asia, and even the mountains of East Africa, which lie almost upon the equator itself (see the map on page 20).

Ice sheets, ice caps, and glaciers may grow or shrink according to the balance of snow accumulation and ice melt. In mountain glaciers, snow accumulates fastest in the higher regions, so the glacier effectively grows from the top (see the illustration above). The increasing weight of ice results in a gradual slippage downslope, where conditions are warmer, so the bottom end of the glacier will be the main area of melting. The Earth's mantle, beneath the crust, is hot and molten, so warmth may arrive at the glacier from the rocks beneath. Ice does not transmit heat well, and its insulating properties mean that the underside of the glacier is warmed and is also a zone of melting. The process of ice loss is called ablation. Whether a particular ice mass is growing or shrinking, therefore, depends upon the balance between accumulation and ablation. This in turn depends upon the climatic conditions and the local topographic setting. Obviously, ablation is at its peak in summertime, while accumulation tends to be greatest in winter, so the overall growth of a glacier is the outcome of the full year's gains and losses. If one could follow the history of a single molecule of water falling on the upper section of a glacier, it would probably go something like this: The molecule would first be compressed into the local ice, then be buried as further snow accumulated. It would then gradually slip downhill through the glacial mass until eventually it emerged at the lower end of the glacier, where it would melt and flow away.

The movement of ice in a glacier is normally very slow, much too slow to be detected by eye. A speed of three feet (1 m) per day is quite fast for a glacier. But occasionally a glacier will accelerate in what is known as a surge. In 1986 one of North America's longest glaciers, the Hubbard Glacier in southern Alaska, suddenly increased its rate of movement to about 33 feet (10 m) per day. It advanced across a bay, crushing the trees on an island in its path and finally colliding with the far side of the bay, where it blocked off a large lake on its landward side. The Hubbard Glacier's acceleration seems to have been caused by a sudden increase in the supply of ice from one of its tributary glaciers as a result of high levels of precipitation. The surging of glaciers is not common but is known to have taken place in Iceland, Greenland, Alaska, and several locations in Russia. It is very unusual in mountain glaciers away from the Arctic, but glacial surges have been recorded in the Andes of South America.

Ice, therefore, like water, flows downhill. The weight of new ice accumulation at the top pushes the entire mass downward. The warming effect produced by the Earth's heat at the junction between the ice and the underlying rock also assists this flow, melting the basal ice and lubricating the base of the glacier. The mass movement of ice in a glacier creates lines of tension and strain. Surface cracking may occur, resulting in the formation of deep cracks that run along the line of movement of the glacier; these cracks are called crevasses. In the lower parts, mass slippage can cause cracks to form at right angles to the direction of movement, called shear lines. Melting at the sides of the glacier and at its lowest point can result in overhangs of ice, and melting beneath the ice can result in the emergence of streams from tunnels, called ice snouts. When light shines through the ice in these more fragmented parts, a vivid blue color may be apparent. This is due to the fact that, although ice reflects much of the light that falls upon it, the spectrum of the light that does penetrate into the ice is mainly absorbed, only blue light being transmitted.

When glaciers or ice sheets flow directly into the ocean, they can form high cliffs of ice and their continued movement into the sea results in spectacular collapses of these ice walls. Whole sections of the ice may break away and be released in floating islands of ice, the icebergs. This process is known as calving because it is almost as though the glacier is giving birth to new, small ice masses. The glaciers of Glacier Bay, Alaska, are best observed from ships offshore, and the region has become a tourist attraction because of its impressive ice cliffs.

*Europe's largest glacier, the Aletsch in central Switzerland. As the glacier moves gently downhill it transports a load of rock detritus on its surface and within the ice.* (Photo by Julian Barkway)

## Effects of glaciation

The high mountain ranges in which many glaciers form are subject to intense erosion, and the resulting rubble, soil, and detritus often ends up on the ice surfaces of the glaciers. It falls from cliffs and slips down slopes, piling onto the stream of gently moving ice in the valley below. Even more eroded material may be gained as the ice scours the ground surface at its base. The heavy mass of ice, slowly grinding its way downhill, carves out rocks and breaks them up under its massive weight. When ablation (the loss of ice by melting) occurs, all of these suspended materials are released once again and may be either deposited on the spot or transported farther by water that has resulted from ice melt, known as *fluvial outwash*. Long after the ice has gone, these deposited materials, often found far from any remaining areas of active glaciers, provide evidence of former glaciation.

Around 5.8 million square miles (15 million km$^2$) of the Earth's land surface, or about 10 percent of the total, is currently covered by ice. Only 22,000 years ago, an area about three times as large was ice-covered. We know this because of the direct and indirect signs the glaciers left when they retreated. Many regions of tundra, both polar and alpine, bear the marks of ice action in the very recent past.

When glaciers grind their way down a valley, they excavate materials in a very characteristic manner (see illustration on opposite page). The floor of the valley becomes smooth and rounded, while the sides of the valley are left steep, so that in section a glaciated valley has a distinctive U shape. The steepened sides may cut back into the side valleys that empty into the main valley, leaving them cut short, or "hanging," often with their streams descending as waterfalls into the main valley. The head of the main valley is often carved out in a steep, rounded, basinlike form, creating what is known as a cirque or corrie. A mountain that has formed the focal point from which several valley glaciers have arisen often remains as a sharpened peak, eroded on all sides, like the famous Matterhorn in Switzerland, while hills carved out by foothill or "piedmont" glaciers are rounded and smooth. Rock faces exposed to passing glaciers may bear scars in the form of parallel lines and scratches caused by the slow grinding of

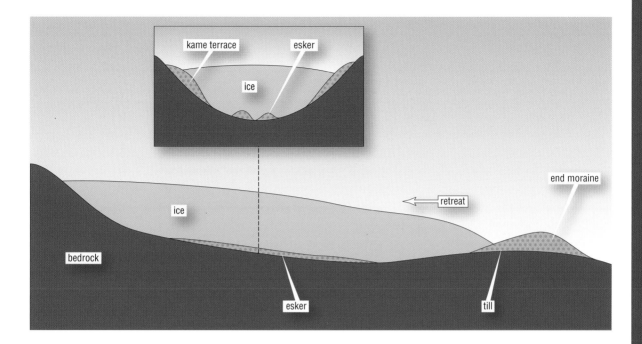

rocks contained in the moving ice. Central Park in New York City has a number of large rocks with such marks upon them, bearing witness to former glaciation in that area. This provides evidence that the tundra biome was once much more extensive on Earth, reaching as far south as modern New York City.

When glaciers retreat, they leave materials behind them that provide further evidence of their former extent and the direction of their movement. The mass of material transported by ice includes large rocks and boulders as well as finely ground detritus, sometimes referred to as "rock flour." When this mix is deposited in an unsorted mass, it is called *till*, or sometimes boulder clay. Much of North America and northern Europe and parts of northern Asia are covered by such tills derived from rocks of the far north, which were carried south by large-scale glacial movements. Many tills are derived from geologically recent glaciations (often occurring during the past 1 million years), but there are also ancient tills from much earlier times. These very ancient tills, usually termed *tillites*, have become consolidated, cemented, and hardened until they have the appearance of a rock. They are

*Cross section of a decaying valley glacier along both its long and short axes. Melting ice at the base of the glacier produces ridges of detritus called* eskers, *and the sides of the glacier retreat to form lateral banks, or kame terraces. At its lowest point, the retreating glacier leaves an end moraine.*

very valuable to geologists because they provide clues to the timing and location of ancient glaciations.

Till may entirely bury the parent rocks of a region, and it may also contain large rock passengers carried from far afield, known as *erratics*. Studied in the context of the geology of surrounding areas, these erratics can provide evidence of the direction of flow of a glacier. Sometimes the rock fragments within a till all point in the same direction, and their orientation can indicate the direction of former ice flow. The same is not true of tills derived from floating ice. When an iceberg melts, it also deposits all of the detritus it contains onto the seabed, but there will be no orientation of stones in a sediment of this type. Sometimes such material contains some microscopic marine fossils, however, and this can help to identify the materials left by sea ice.

Glacial advances and retreats are determined by the climate and its effect on the accumulation/ablation balance of the ice mass. A glacier may remain static for a time, perhaps a few decades or even centuries, and then undergo retreat, in which case it often leaves behind a distinct ridge of till marking its

*A glacier in retreat near Obergurgl, Austria, has left behind a terminal moraine of rock detritus, which is being eroded and sorted by the flow of water from melting ice.* (Photo by Peter D. Moore)

terminal position. Called a *moraine*, this feature often has a profound effect upon the future development of the landscape. If it blocks the flow of water from the melting glacier or from the stream that succeeds it, it can result in the formation of a lake. Many lakes in regions formerly glaciated have been created in this way. The formation of these moraine lakes greatly diversifies the glaciated landscape, as can be seen in the Sierra Nevada of California, where Convict Lake is an excellent example of a moraine glacial lake. The sediments that accumulate within these lakes provide a record of the climatic, vegetation, and other environmental changes that took place during the course of the lake's history.

As well as being deposited at the terminus of a glacier, till may also build up beneath the ice, in which case the piles of deposited material take on a distinctive, streamlined form, aligned to the direction of glacial flow (see the illustration on page 41). These formations, called *drumlins*, become apparent when the ice melts. Isolated patches of ice left behind on level valley floors and plateaus, called dead ice, melt to release an amorphous, randomly scattered series of piles of till called hummocky moraine. Finally, single blocks of ice buried in till melt slowly to form deep, steep-sided hollows that often fill with water to form kettle-hole lakes. The pothole wetlands of the prairie regions of North America have developed from the infilling of kettle-hole lakes.

## After the ice

Clearly, when changes in climate cause glaciers to retreat, they leave behind many clues to their former presence, marks on the landscape that tell a geologist that ice has been present in the past. But the impact of the ice itself is not the only clue. Glacial melt not only deposits detritus but also releases large volumes of water, so it is inevitable that much of the material resulting from glacial activity is washed and sorted by water flow. While the glacier is still intact, streams form within the very body of the ice, and these ice-confined streams sort the detritus into long, sinuous ridges called *eskers*. These can be up to 100 feet (30 m) in height and remain distinctive long after the ice has departed. Along the edges of the glacier, meltwater can create similar strips of sorted material that form terraces on the valley side. These are termed *kame terraces*. Downstream of the glacier, deposited detritus continues to be sorted by meltwater flow, forming "braided" streams running in a series of parallel ribbons, their waters often milky in appearance because of the high content of clay resulting from glacial erosion.

Water is not the only means by which glacial detritus can be further transported and sorted; the wind is also an active agent. When water carries and sorts the different sizes of particles that emerge from glaciers, the particles become deposited in a series of narrow, parallel ridges in the riverbed, called *braided ridges*, and there they dry out. Once the particles that form the ridges are dry, the strong winds that often occur in the vicinity of a glacier pick up the finer sediments and carry them over great distances before depositing them in new locations. Since the rivers provide a constant source of this material, the wind may carry large quantities and deposit them all together, forming a silty or sandy loess soil. Loess soils are therefore rich in fine particles. Because they are formed from freshly ground rock, they are also rich in chemical nutrients, so they produce very fertile ground. Loess soils are particularly frequent in Alaska, in central Europe (from Belgium to Ukraine), and in China. The great agricultural regions of the American Midwest are based upon loess soils.

Fossils are, not surprisingly, scarce in glacial deposits. The degree of physical damage and abrasion precludes the survival of most biological material. Apart from that, glacial landscapes do not normally support large numbers of animals and plants. Occasionally, however, the bones of large mammals survive in glacial outwash, along with other very resistant materials, such as the wing cases of beetles. In rare instances, pockets of peaty soils are preserved, containing plant fragments usually of Arctic-alpine vegetation. Caves around the glaciers are also good sources of fossils, because animals, including humans, often used these for shelter and remains may have accumulated on the cave floor. The deposits build up over the course of years in a sequence of layers, the deepest being the oldest. Cave deposits can thus provide evidence of the biological history of a glaciated region over the course of time.

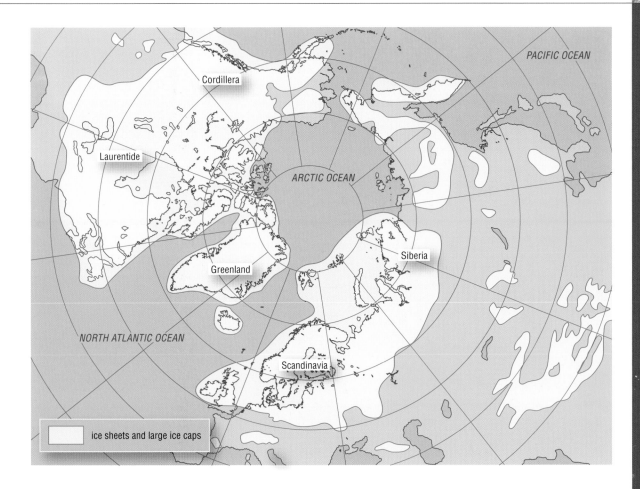

*The maximum extent of ice sheets and glaciers in the Northern Hemisphere during the most recent ice age*

By studying these various glacial features and their marks upon the landscape, glacial geologists have been able to put together detailed pictures of former glaciation events. Answering the seemingly simple question of how many glaciations have taken place in recent times, however, has been made difficult by the fact that the latest glaciation has often destroyed or obscured the evidence of former glacial events. The glacial features themselves are relatively easy to recognize, but deciding exactly when they were produced, and in what sequence, is much more difficult. Geologists have mapped the extent of ice when the last ice age was at its maximum, around 22,000 to 20,000 years ago, and the map above shows this extent in the Northern Hemisphere. Many of the regions covered by the ice sheets had been glaciated during former cold episodes over the past million years, but much of the evidence for these earlier glaciations was destroyed by this final ice advance.

## Patterns on the ground

The region around the edge of a glacier following glacial retreat is called the *periglacial region*. The conditions here are cold but not quite cold enough to support a year-round ice cover. Even when ice has retreated from an area, leaving bare rock and glacial debris, ice may remain beneath the surface of the ground. This happens especially in polar regions but also occurs in some high parts of the world such as Tibet and Mongolia. If the mean annual temperature remains below the freezing point of water, then water below the ground may remain in a frozen state. The surface water, however, is warmed by the Sun and remains in a liquid state through the brief summer, so a wet soil overlies permanent ice. Permanently frozen subsoil is called *permafrost*. Regions affected in this way are conveniently divided into two types: continuous permafrost, in which there is an uninterrupted layer of permanently frozen soil beneath the ground; and discontinuous permafrost, where frozen soil is patchy and interspersed with areas that seasonally defrost. The map on page 47 shows the geographical distribution of permafrost. It is in the southern, warmer regions, usually occupied by coniferous forest rather than tundra, that permafrost becomes sporadic. Where it is discontinuous, the remaining patches of permafrost tend to be confined to the more exposed ridges where protective blankets of snow fail to accumulate in winter. The depth of the permafrost is variable, but it can be very deep. Records from Canada suggest that permafrost can extend to two-thirds of a mile (1 km) in depth.

The map shows the areas of both discontinuous and continuous permafrost, and it can be seen that the true tundra regions (shown in the map on page 2) fall mainly within the area of continuous permafrost. The permafrost map also shows locations of permanent offshore ice, which are really the oceanic equivalent of permafrost, since the waters remain frozen at all times of the year. Observe that the areas of permafrost extend farthest south in areas with the most continental climates, as in Siberia. Note also the large block of discontinuous permafrost well to the south of the main permafrost distribution in the highlands of Tibet. These regions are very far from any ocean and therefore cannot be heated by the influence of warm oceanic currents. Landmasses also lose heat faster than the oceans, so the interiors of continents tend to experience low winter temperatures. In the case of the highlands of Tibet, the high altitude (most of the land is higher than 12,000 feet [3,600 m]) also contributes to the low temperatures. The influence of the warm ocean currents moving northward in the North Atlantic (shown in the map on page 12) is also clear in this map. Northern Europe is clear of continuous permafrost because of the warming effect of these ocean currents, despite the fact that it lies as far north

*The extent of continuous and discontinuous permafrost in the Northern Hemisphere*

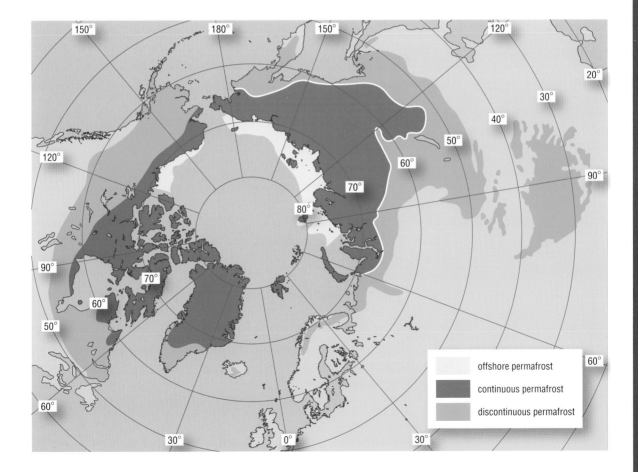

offshore permafrost

continuous permafrost

discontinuous permafrost

as much of Siberia and Canada. No warm currents penetrate to these regions, so these lands are locked in permafrost.

The surface of the ground is strongly affected by the cycle of freeze and thaw of the soils above the permafrost. This upper layer of soil, which is defrosted each spring, is called the *active layer*. It is within this layer of the soil that most physical, chemical, and biological soil processes take place. The plant roots are confined to this layer. Plant roots often occupy only the very uppermost levels (about the top four inches [10 cm]) of the soil but may extend down to about 10 inches (25 cm) in places. The depth of the active layer depends on a number of factors, including the nature of the soil. In flat meadow soils, only the top 12 to 17 inches (30 to 40 cm) may thaw in summer, while on drier sites the thaw may extend to a depth of about three feet (1 m). If there is a layer of organic litter or wet peat over the mineral soil (which is often the case), this insulates the soil against the spring warming and the active layer remains very shallow.

When water freezes it expands, exerting pressure on any object in contact with it. As winter commences, the water contained within the deeper layers of soil, which are in contact with the permafrost, begins to freeze. The temperature of the surface soil, which is exposed to the cold night air, also falls rapidly and the water it holds also freezes. The layer of wet, unfrozen soil sandwiched between the upper and lower ice zones is consequently placed under pressure because the soils above and below are expanding. The result is that bubbles of wet soil may burst through the surface of the ground, releasing a mass of muddy material over the local vegetation. Where this happens, the surface of the tundra becomes patchy, with bare soil areas often raised above their surroundings by the pressures from below.

The great pressure exerted from below by the wet soil, expanding as it freezes, forces any stones or rock fragments in the soil up toward the surface. This forcing of rocks to the surface is called *frost heaving*. The reason why stones in particular are pushed upward through the soil is that they lose heat more rapidly than their surrounding soil. Stones conduct heat well, so they quickly become hot or cold under the right conditions. This is why stones feel hot to the touch in the sunshine but very cold at night. As a result of this property of the stones, the soil around them (particularly the soil immediately below them) becomes cold faster, and this is where water begins to freeze. The expansion that results from this freezing pushes the stones upward through the soil and they end up on the surface.

Larger stones are usually forced upward more effectively than small stones, so the frost sorts the rocks into different sizes. Moreover, when rocks and stones are brought to the surface, they are not randomly spaced but often develop in patterns. This results from the fact that the stones move sideways as well as upward. On flat ground, the stones become arranged in a kind of network called *stone polygons.* Why they should form a network is a question best answered by considering what happens when a pool of water dries out: Even in temperate climates, the exposed mud usually becomes caked and cracked in a distinct pattern of polygons. These usually six-sided shapes form because of the way in which soils dry out and contract. Similarly, in tundra habitats the freezing and thawing of the ground causes the soil to contract periodically into polygons, and the stones on their way up through the soil move into the cracks on the surface, forming stone polygons. On a slope, these polygons are narrower, and on steep slopes they form a linear series of *stone stripes,* aligned along the contours. These stone patterns on the surface of the ground can still be detected in regions now far from the tundra, such as New England and southern Britain, indicating that these regions once experienced periglacial conditions.

Another feature of periglacial regions is the formation of ice wedges in the soil (see the illustration on page 50). When soil freezes, it forms cracks over its surface and, as described, these often take on the form of a network of polygons, looking rather like a honeycomb from the air. Water abounds in low-lying regions of the tundra because evaporation is low in the cool temperatures, and it fills these cracks and then freezes and expands in winter, pushing the cracks deeper into the soil and widening them in the process. In cross section, the water that freezes within these cracks looks like a wedge that is driven into the soil, so these features are called *ice wedges.* They are widest at the surface of the ground, where more water is added each summer, and narrowest at their deepest tip. The resulting patterned landscape takes on the form of *ice-wedge polygons,* and these cover many areas of the tundra landscape. The center of the polygon may be raised into a dry crest, or it may become sunken and bear a pool of water during the summer, so that the center and the edges of the polygon bear different vegetation, emphasizing the pattern further. The wedges themselves thaw out in summer and form an interconnecting web of narrow waterways, and these become filled with aquatic vegetation and then silt as the surrounding soils become eroded into the channels.

Ice-wedge polygons will form only under very cold conditions, usually with a mean annual temperature of 21°F (–6°C) or lower. They can occur in a fossil state in lands far south of their current distribution, indicating that very low temperatures prevailed in that region in the past. The size of the polygons is variable, from a few feet to as much as 300 feet (100 m)

*Some of the geological features found in Arctic tundra. Ice lenses below the ground surface may expand to form large mounds called* pingos. *Ice can also penetrate the soil from the surface, often forming ice wedges that are arranged in polygonal patterns.*

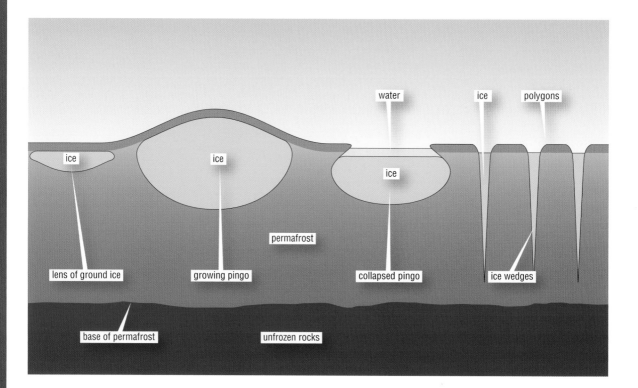

in diameter. When the perimeter becomes slightly raised above the center because of the expansion of the ice wedge, which forces up the sediments in the crack, then the depressed middle of the polygon may become an open pool of water (see the illustrations on page 52).

Patterns of stone stripes and polygons are also found in alpine situations where the conditions are cold enough. Even on the summits of the equatorial mountains in East Africa, polygons can be found, but here they are much smaller, often only four to eight inches (10 to 20 cm) across. They are formed by the same basic mechanisms as their polar counterparts, but the freezing and thawing is due to the difference in day and night temperatures rather than any difference in season. Perhaps this is why their development is on so much smaller a scale.

In some periglacial regions, huge mounds (perhaps even several hundred feet in height and diameter) may rise out of an otherwise flat landscape. These are especially frequent in the coastal plain of Alaska and in the coastal zone of eastern Greenland. These structures, called *pingos,* often develop over dried-out lake basins or along the sides of streams and rivers. Pingos become elevated by the growth of an ice core in the center of the mound, formed as a result of water pressure from below. Usually they develop in the sites where springs of water rise from the ground under pressure and feed the ice core, which freezes as it nears the surface of the ground. The upper part of the mound has a very different microclimate from the surrounding lowlands, and the southern slopes of the pingo mound may bear vegetation characteristic of a warmer climate, possibly even a tree cover. If the general climate becomes warmer, however, the ice core in the center of the pingo melts and the whole mass collapses to form a deep pool, surrounded by a circular rim or "rampart" formed from the soil and other detritus raised up by the mound. Circular ponds with ramparts can be found far to the south of the present-day tundra regions, indicating the periglacial conditions that once prevailed there (see the illustration on opposite page).

A similar type of structure is sometimes formed in those regions of the Arctic that are rich in peat bogs, and this is

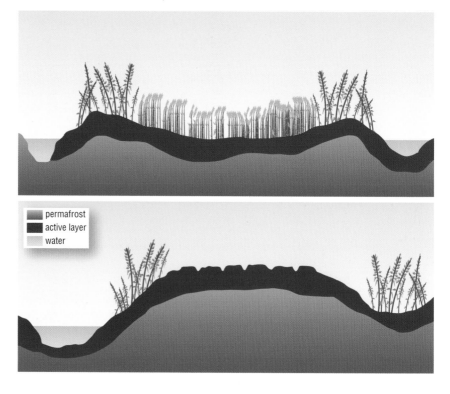

Profiles of Arctic polygons, showing both the low-centered and the high-centered forms. The active layer of the surface soil melts each spring, while the deeper layers (permafrost) remain frozen. Low-centered polygons bear marsh vegetation, while high-centered forms are dry and covered only with mosses and lichens.

permafrost
active layer
water

termed a *palsa*. Palsas, like pingos, are large mounds that are formed by the development of ice beneath the surface of the ground. Generally smaller than pingos, palsas are only six to 10 feet (2 to 3 m) in height and about 150 feet (45 m) across. They often lie within wetland areas, where they are interspersed with open pools and other palsas in various states of development. Palsas begin their formation as small irregularities on the surface of a sedge marsh. Even a very small elevation of an inch or two can affect snow accumulation. The snow is blown from the slight mound and accumulates in the hollows between, so the more elevated spots have less snow cover in the winter. They therefore become colder, because snow acts as an insulating blanket, retaining some of the ground's heat that it gained in the summer sun. By contrast, the cold penetrates any small raised areas of ground, causing an ice core to develop within them (as shown in the illustrations on pages 50, 52, and 54). As the ice forms, it expands, pushing the hummock even higher so that even less snow is retained in the high winds. Palsa growth is thus a self-propagating process: The higher the palsa grows the colder it becomes, and the colder it becomes the more the ice core expands and pushes the palsa upward. The ice core survives through the summer, so its growth continues for many years, even centuries.

As the palsa grows in height, drainage improves and the vegetation on its surface becomes drier. The surface of the palsa may then develop a vegetation cover of lichens. Many lichens are white or pale gray, and these reflect the sunlight, keeping the mound cool in summer. In the course of time, dwarf shrubs replace these lichens, but these have a darker color and absorb more heat from the summer sun. This, coupled with the increasing height of the dome, eventually leads to erosion of the surface soil, revealing the peat beneath. The dark-colored peat absorbs even more heat, and its exposure leads to the meltdown of the ice core. The core collapses quite quickly, leading to the formation of an open pool of water that is available for recolonization by sedges as the cycle begins again. Finnish scientists, working in the 1980s, demonstrated experimentally how this process operates. They spent a whole winter visiting an area of Arctic sedge bog where, using a broom, they swept an area clear of snow and kept it clear through the winter. The result was the development of a permanent ice core beneath the ground, and within a few years the swept locality was developing into a palsa.

All of these structures associated with tundra environments lead to a diversity of landscapes and landforms. This is very important when one considers the range of microhabitats that are available for the plants and animals that inhabit the inhospitable world of the tundra. The mounds and hollows, wetlands and drylands, slopes and cliffs all offer opportunities for living things to find a home, survive, and breed. As will become clear, the biodiversity of the tundra is not high, but such richness as it contains is due largely to the diversity of its landscape features. Geology, or more strictly, geomorphology, plays an important role in the maintenance of the tundra's biodiversity.

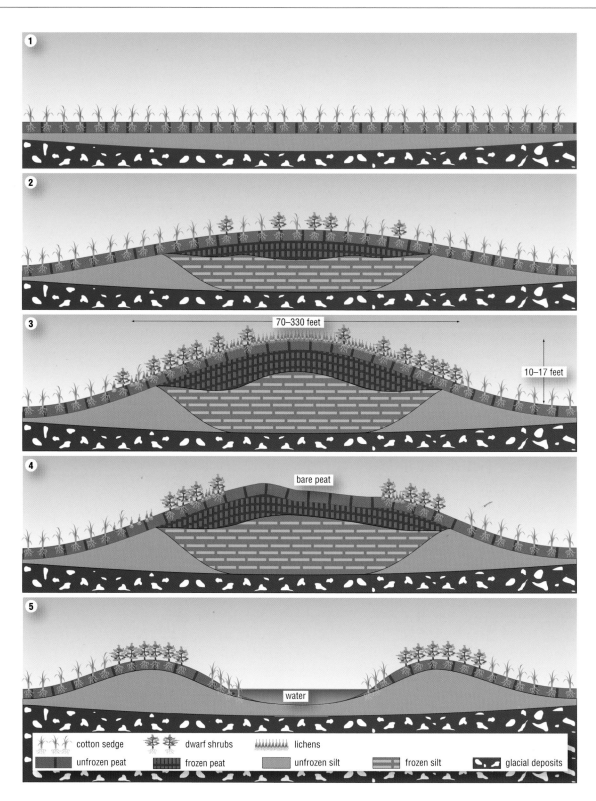

1

2

3
70–330 feet
10–17 feet

4
bare peat

5
water

cotton sedge        dwarf shrubs        lichens
unfrozen peat        frozen peat        unfrozen silt        frozen silt        glacial deposits

## Soil formation in the tundra

As has been described, in areas of permafrost, the deeper parts of soils are frozen throughout the year while the upper layers melt during the summer. The result of this annual drastic change is that soil conditions are also altered strongly from one season to another. The formation of ice means that soils are constantly being heaved, stirred, contorted, and disturbed, leading to a degree of instability. On slopes, the upper layer is likely to become highly mobile in summer as the wet surface soil slides over the top of the frozen lower layers. Soil slips downhill and gathers at the base in a process called *solifluction*. Even on level ground, soils in effect plow themselves as stones are heaved upward to the surface, resulting in a constant mixing of the upper layers. As they move, these stones are fragmented by the activity of frost and mechanical damage.

All soils throughout the world are produced initially by the breakdown of rocks into small fragments. This process, called *weathering*, results from the action of physical and biological factors on the rock. In the tundra, the action of freezing and thawing is particularly important because the penetration of ice into rock surfaces can split them into sections so that the rock decays under the stress. This is particularly apparent when rocks and cliff faces are directly exposed to the air, where the changes in temperature are strongest. Freezing and thawing causes rock falls and generates masses of rock rubble, known as *tallus scree,* on the slopes beneath the cliffs. This is particularly obvious in mountain regions, and rock breakdown may be particularly active in summer in alpine sites. The very hot summer of 2003 in the European Alps led to pronounced rock falls and even led to the closure for safety reasons of one of the favorite peaks for mountaineers, the Matterhorn in Switzerland. In winter, snow avalanches are often the greatest danger to humans on mountains. They are also a major contributor to rock breakage and destruction.

(opposite page) *The development of palsas. Ice forms beneath the tundra soil surface and expands to build a mound. The elevated surface dries, leading to changing vegetation and eventually to erosion, when the palsa collapses to form a pool.*

Within tundra soils, rock weathering takes place primarily in the active layer, where thawing and refreezing take place each year. Deeper in the soil, in the permafrost, such temperature changes do not occur and the underlying rocks remain below freezing. The outcome is that physical weathering occurs mainly above ground or within the active layer of the soil. This may not be as spectacular as the large-scale rock breaking that occurs on cliff faces, but it is nevertheless an important process. Rock particles are split into smaller portions by water that penetrates into cracks and freezes. Over the course of time, the chemicals contained within the rocks are released after being trapped in the rocks for many millions of years, and they become available to the living plants within the ecosystem once more.

In addition to physical breakdown, weathering can also result from biological activities, in which living organisms assist in the breakdown of rocks. Lichens on the surface of exposed rocks, for example, actively attack the rock by secreting acidic compounds that dissolve the rock surface beneath them. This can strip away flakes of rock in a process called *exfoliation.* Algae may likewise coat the surface of the rock. Grazing mollusks such as snails that eat algae and lichens may then scrape the rock itself with their rasping tongues. Plant roots, including those of dwarf willows (*Salix* species) and the mountain avens (*Dryas octopetala*), may penetrate cracks in rocks and enlarge them as the roots grow and expand. The force exerted by roots extending as they forage for water and minerals in the ground is entirely adequate for the splitting of rocks.

Although physical weathering of rock occurs relatively quickly in the tundra, biological and chemical weathering take place rather slowly. The chemical reactions in the soil that assist in the breakdown of rocks, such as the impact of acids from the atmosphere on the soil particles, are slower in the tundra than in the Tropics because of the low temperature, so chemical weathering is slow. The action of bacteria and fungi in the soil produces corrosive materials that attack both mineral and organic matter, but this process is also slower in the tundra or restricted to those limited times in the year when the temperature is high enough to allow bacterial and fungal growth. So, although freezing and thawing have a strong impact on rock weathering, the more subtle action of chemicals and soil organisms is slow.

The limited activity of bacteria and fungi in the soil means that organic matter produced by the dead portions of plants does not decay rapidly. Consequently, soils may develop reserves of organic material. In the wetter locations this organic matter may even accumulate as peat. Organic matter is good at holding water, like a sponge, so it prevents many tundra soils from becoming excessively dry in summer. It is also efficient at holding the scarce mineral elements that plants require for their nutrition, so that the peat forms an important reserve of elements within the soil. Most rocks of the Arctic are relatively poor in the chemicals needed by plants. Phosphorus and nitrogen, in particular, are in short supply. The low level of precipitation also means that relatively little in the way of chemical input arrives from the atmosphere (see "Nutrient cycling in the tundra," pages 76–81).

## Soil types of the tundra

It is possible to divide tundra soils into two main types, "skeletal soils" and peaty soils. The skeletal soils, so called because they consist mainly of rock fragments of various sizes and very little organic matter, develop in well-drained sites, such as on the tops of esker ridges. Here vegetation is sparse and the limited precipitation from the atmosphere passes quickly through the soil, moving down the slopes to the water-accumulating regions in the valleys and on the plains. Within these wetter locations decomposition is inhibited by the abundance of water, and so organic matter does not rot away but develops as peat over the mineral soil.

Skeletal soils, sometimes called "rankers," are found where the process of rock weathering has produced masses of fragments but where the long-term effects of vegetation development and the percolation of water have not taken place. In a sense, they can be regarded as young or immature soils. They have the basic mineral components but lack the full range of animals, plants, and microbes that are found in a fully developed mature soil. As these additional components arrive, and as the constant downward movement of water through the soil takes place, the soil develops a distinct series of layers, called *horizons.* The orderly series of horizons within a soil is known as its *profile.* The profile of a soil is its cross section, and soil scientists usually view it by digging a pit right down to the underlying rock (see photograph on opposite page). In the skeletal soils, the soil profile is very simple, consisting of broken rock overlying the basal rock or the ice of the permafrost. The underlying basal rock is often the source of the fragments that make up the soil, so it is called the parent material. Skeletal soils are found where glaciers have recently retreated or on slopes and dry ridges, often with little or no vegetation cover.

In the shrub tundra of the Low Arctic, where vegetation forms a continuous cover, the soil may mature to form a more complex profile. The surface vegetation of this region, consisting of plants belonging to the blueberry and heather family (Ericaceae), produces a very acid litter as the dead leaves of these plants fall to the ground. This litter of dead plant material usually accumulates as a layer of slowly decomposing organic matter, called *humus,* on the soil surface. The mineral soil below this humus consists of two distinct layers: an upper pale, bleached layer, and a darker, reddish colored lower layer. The organic top cover and the bleached layer are termed the A horizon and the lower red layer is the B horizon. There is a lower subsoil called the C horizon, which is really just decomposing rock, often lying within the permafrost. A soil with this layered, or stratified, profile is called a *podzol.* It is very common in the boreal forest (or taiga) zone, but also extends into the southern parts of the tundra where there is an extensive dwarf-shrub vegetation cover. The A horizon of a podzol is usually acidic and poor in nutrients, so the development of this type of soil profile has an impact on the vegetation and consequently on the animals that graze upon it.

The conditions needed to produce the layers of a podzol are quite complicated. Water from melting snow or summer rain moves downward through the soil under the influence of gravity. As it passes through the organic litter layer, the

*The profile of a soil developing over a bedrock of chalk. The disintegrating rock at the base is overlain by smaller rock fragments mixed with organic matter derived from the surface vegetation.* (Photo by Peter D. Moore)

water picks up various organic chemicals, including some called polyphenols, which are derived from the breakdown of the plant tissues. These acidic compounds help to dissolve many of the inorganic chemicals in the upper layers of the

*A podzol soil profile from northern Finland. The surface layer consists of organic litter derived from the vegetation, below which is a pale layer that has been leached of its iron. Lower in the profile is a deposition layer containing iron, aluminum, and organic matter leached from above.* (Photo by Peter D. Moore)

soil, including iron and aluminum, and they also cause fine clay particles to become mobile and to migrate down the soil profile. All of these moving materials become deposited in the lower B horizon, where they form a dark reddish zone, mainly because of the color of the iron oxides present. This type of soil profile is dependent on the downward movement of water, so it can develop only if there is relatively free drainage of water through the soil.

When drainage is poor, as when a site is low-lying and receives an inflow of water from surrounding areas, the soil underneath is often permanently waterlogged and this strongly affects its chemistry and its biology. Poor drainage also affects its general appearance. Digging a pit in such a waterlogged Arctic site would reveal, first, a black layer of poorly decayed organic matter, and below it, a mineral soil, often with a blue-gray appearance. Such a soil is called a *gley*

*soil.* The reason for its gray color is the fact that it is starved of oxygen. Most healthy soils have air spaces within them and the penetration of air into the soil allows oxygen to reach the bacteria, fungi, earthworms, plant roots, and other living organisms that dwell in the soil and depend on oxygen to breathe. When a soil becomes fully saturated with water, all air spaces and channels to the surface become blocked by standing water and the air can no longer penetrate to the lower layers. Although oxygen does dissolve in water and can move by diffusion through water, its rate of movement when dissolved in water is about 10,000 times slower than is possible in the air. So, in a water-soaked environment oxygen is often in very short supply, and this means that microbes, animals, and plant roots are all starved of oxygen. Many plants and animals literally drown in such a difficult habitat.

The dearth of oxygen also affects chemical processes. Some chemical reactions in soils are dependent on oxygen, especially reactions involving the element iron. Iron is a very common element in all soils, and in a well-aerated soil it is usually present in the oxidized form iron-III (ferric iron). Iron-III is often further combined with oxygen to form iron oxides that have a reddish (rusty) color, and this often gives a soil its rich, dark color. When oxygen is in short supply, however, as in gley soils, iron becomes reduced to its iron-II form (ferrous iron). In the iron-II form, the element takes on a blue-gray color that is very apparent in the gley soil profile. So the waterlogged soils of the tundra take on the gray character of the form of iron contained in an oxygen-poor environment.

A careful examination of a gley soil profile will sometimes reveal flecks or lines of reddish color. These rusty spots and stripes are usually associated with the channels and tubes through which roots of plants have penetrated: Old root channels in which the root has died and decayed form access routes for air into the soil. They create tubes along which oxygen can travel, and its presence is displayed by the formation of iron-III oxides with their characteristic rust color.

*Debris from glacial retreat near Lech in Austria has been colonized by herbaceous vegetation. Some shrubs are beginning to invade the developing soils.*
(Photo by Peter D. Moore)

## Soil change in time

Soils change over the course of time, and this is particularly apparent where glaciers retreat and leave areas of ground-up rock behind them that will gradually develop into soils. Indeed, some of the most important scientific studies of soil development have been associated with glacial retreat sites, especially where the timing of the glacial movements has been recorded and where a timescale can therefore be used as a framework for soil development. The process of ecosystem development and maturation involves an array of plants and animals, and the arrival and growth of organisms at a site causes changes in the tundra soil (whether polar or alpine) as it develops.

The soil deposited by a retreating glacier is essentially a mass of rock particles ground down by ice action, perhaps sorted by water movements, and eventually deposited in a site where it becomes physically stable. This is a typical ranker or skeletal soil, poor in organic matter. Any larger rocks remaining become colonized by lichens, and these further corrode the solid materials, producing smaller particles that settle on the soil below. Many lichens are also able to "fix" nitrogen from the air (see "Nutrient cycling in the tundra," pages 76–81), and these play a part in providing a plant nutrient that is essential to all living organisms. Plants can then begin to colonize the soil, and as they thrive and ultimately die they add organic matter to the soil. This is because when a plant dies, a proportion of the living material it produced by photosynthesis is deposited in the soil, where it changes the soil's very nature. The organic matter acts as a sponge and holds water, making the soil a moister place where more plants can grow. It also supplies an energy source for animals such as springtails and earthworms that feed upon dead vegetable matter. The organic humus component of the soil is also very effective at holding various minerals in the soil (such as calcium and potassium) so that

*Dwarf shrubs colonize an area of glacial retreat at the Kangshung Glacier, east of Mount Everest in Tibet.* (Photo by Colin Monteach/ Minden Pictures)

they are not lost but remain as a reservoir available to plants for their growth.

Some mineral elements, however, are inevitably lost. As water drains through the soil profile, it dissolves some of the elements released from the decaying rock particles and carries them away in the drainage water that leaves the soil. This loss of elements is called *leaching*. Some of the chemicals dissolved in rainwater assist in this process, especially acids such as carbonic acid and sulfuric acid that result from the uptake of carbon dioxide and oxides of sulfur respectively from the atmosphere. Plants themselves may also contribute to the speed of leaching, as in the case of podzol development (see "Soil types of the tundra," pages 57–61).

The gradual development of a soil is accompanied by changes in local vegetation and animal life, so it leads the entire ecosystem along a track of growth. Exactly which plants and animals manage to invade and take up residence, depends, of course, on the climatic factors that apply in any given location. Colonization of the soil by dwarf shrubs of the Ericaceae family can lead to the development of podzol soils on the better-drained sites. Where conditions are wetter and drainage poor, then the peaty soils and gleys develop. So the tundra region bears a variety of soils and these change both in space and in time.

## The tundra atmosphere

All soil processes, from the weathering of rocks to the formation of peat, are affected by the air above the surface and within the pores of the soil structure. The soil has an atmosphere of its own, which interacts and exchanges gases with the atmosphere above. Precipitation passes through the atmosphere and gathers some chemicals as it falls toward the ground, so the atmosphere can supply elements to the soil in this way. The vegetation that grows upon the surface of the soil and adds organic matter to its structure derives the element of carbon from the atmosphere in photosynthesis. To understand the chemistry of tundra environments, therefore, it is necessary to know something of the atmosphere above the ground.

The Earth is surrounded by the *atmosphere,* a layer of gases held close to the planet by its gravitational pull. The most abundant gas is nitrogen, composing about 79 percent of the atmosphere. This is a relatively nonreactive gas, and although nitrogen is vital to all living organisms as a component of proteins, the gaseous nitrogen of the atmosphere can be tapped only by a small number of microbes. Of the remaining 21 percent of the atmosphere, the bulk is made up of oxygen, which is, of course, vital for *respiration.* Together with most animals and plants, people take in oxygen and use it in a controlled combustion in their cells to release energy; this is called respiration. Atmospheric oxygen used in respiration is replenished by green plants, which produce oxygen as a waste product of their activities in photosynthesis. A very small proportion of the atmosphere is occupied by carbon dioxide (less than 0.04 percent), water vapor, and various trace gases. These smaller components of the atmosphere are important because some of them have the ability to absorb and retain heat energy. They create a kind of thermal blanket around the Earth that absorbs the heat radiated from the Earth and maintains a fairly stable set of conditions at the Earth's surface. Human disturbance of this balance of scarcer gases and the way in which such disturbance affects the tundra are problems that are becoming increasingly urgent (see "Tundra as a carbon sink," pages 172–173).

The atmosphere is densest close to the surface of the Earth because of the pressure of gases above it. But Earth's atmosphere is considerably less dense than that of some other planets, such as Venus, where a high concentration of carbon dioxide produces an atmospheric pressure roughly 90 times that of the Earth. The atmosphere becomes thinner with increasing height above the surface of the Earth, and it is convenient to divide it into various layers according to its composition and properties. The lowermost layer, which extends up to a height of about seven miles (11 km), is the *troposphere.* Most meteorological activity takes place here; clouds, even the highest cirrus ice clouds, are mainly located within this layer. As explained earlier, temperature decreases with increasing height within the troposphere (see the sidebar "Lapse rate," page 19), but at the very top of this layer a change occurs at a point called the *tropopause.* Just above the tropopause is the *stratosphere,* and this layer extends up to a height of about 31 miles (50 km). The stratosphere contains significant quantities of ozone, and this gas has properties that are of particular importance to the polar tundra regions. Ozone absorbs solar radiation in the ultraviolet (UV) part of the spectrum. As a result, parts of the stratosphere actually become warmer than the upper layers of the troposphere, sometimes reaching as high as 50°F (10°C). Most of the light that is visible at the surface of the Earth and that plants use in photosynthesis passes through the stratosphere, but the very short wavelength energy of UV is absorbed by the stratospheric ozone and filtered out. This is important to all the living things on the land surfaces of the Earth because high-energy UV radiation is potentially damaging to cell structure. It causes breakdown of various cell components, including the DNA, which carries genetic information, and this damage can lead to cell malfunction and even cancer, especially of the skin. So the ozone of the stratosphere is critical for the protection of life on Earth. In the tundra regions, especially of the Antarctic, stratospheric ozone destruction has been noted in recent years and this is a cause of concern (see "Ozone holes," pages 178–180). What happens in the polar atmosphere can provide an early warning for those parts of the world where human populations are denser and may be in danger.

Another essential aspect of the polar atmosphere relates to the layers that lie above the stratosphere. From a height of 31 miles (50 km) to about 50 miles (80 km) lies a layer called the *mesosphere,* at the top of which the temperature may be around –180°F (–120°C). The density of the atmosphere here is very low, but it still contains enough oxygen to burn up the meteorites that head toward the Earth, creating shooting stars. Above this, up to around 250 miles (400 km), lies the thermosphere, where the atmosphere gradually thins to the emptiness of space. Satellites are positioned at around this altitude. It is also in this layer that a remarkable polar phenomenon, the *aurora,* takes place. This consists of flickering sheets of light that pass across the night sky in the very high latitudes in both the Northern and Southern Hemispheres. In the north this is known as the aurora borealis (*Boreas* is Greek for "north wind"), or "northern lights," and in the south the aurora australis (*Auster* is Latin for "south wind"). These spectacular displays occur when the molecules of the thin upper atmosphere are bombarded by charged particles emitted by the Sun, known as the *solar wind.* The reason why auroras are restricted to the polar regions is that the magnetic poles attract and concentrate the charged particles of the solar wind. The intensity of particles emitted from the Sun varies with the activity of the Sun in the form of sunspots. When a solar flare takes place on the surface of the Sun, spectacular displays of the aurora occur about 24 hours later. Sometimes these polar displays can be seen as far south as the northern United States or in England. Their occurrence makes the atmosphere above the polar tundra of particular interest to atmospheric physicists.

## Conclusions

The cold conditions of the regions surrounding the North and the South Poles have encouraged the accumulation of permanent ice sheets. Mobile masses of ice in the form of glaciers have also developed both in polar and some mountainous regions of the world, and the presence of ice has had a major impact on the physical environment of the tundra. Over long periods of time ice can grind away mountains and create valleys. When ice melts it deposits detritus that creates a variety of distinctive landforms. Ice in the soil, the permafrost, is also responsible for the development of patterned ground and strange geological blisters called pingos and palsas. Soils in the tundra are often unstable because the freezing and thawing processes place them under great stress, but in time tundra soils mature to produce distinctively layered profiles, and this maturation is accompanied by the invasion and stabilization of tundra vegetation.

Above the Earth, the polar atmosphere is the location of one of the most spectacular light displays to be found on the planet. It is hardly surprising, then, that the tundra environment has attracted close attention from both geologists and atmospheric physicists.

# CHAPTER 3

# THE TUNDRA ECOSYSTEM

For thousands of years, naturalists have studied the structure of different plants and animals and the ways in which they resemble one another. They have observed how living things grow, move, and reproduce and how they are distributed over the surface of the Earth. As a result of these studies, scientists in the 19th century, particularly Charles Darwin but also many others, began to ask questions about how species interact with one another and how they respond to the physical environment, including the climate and the soil. The study of the ways in which organisms relate to their surroundings, both biological and physical, is called *ecology*. Central to the science of ecology is the concept of the *ecosystem*.

## What is an ecosystem?

Living organisms can be looked upon in many different ways. The simplest approach is to study the individual: its structure, its biochemistry, or its behavior. But individuals usually occur in groups, and to understand the individual it is sensible to study it in the context of the other members of its species. A group of individuals of the same species is called a population, and individuals usually modify their behavior to fit in with the other members of the population. In nature, however, pure populations of a single species are unusual; more frequently different species are found mixed up together. A collection of individuals belonging to a number of different species is called a community. When different species are mixed together in this way, they interact. One species may eat or may act as a parasite upon another. Some species demand the same resources from their surroundings and find themselves in competition with one another. Some species may even inadvertently aid one another, as when a fern grows in the shade and protection of a tree, or when a bee, as it collects nectar, accidentally carries pollen from one flower to another. All kinds of interaction are possible between species in a community.

One further component is involved in the ecosystem, and that is the physical environment. The ecosystem includes all of the living organisms found in a location (the community) plus all of the nonliving materials and factors that form their background (including the chemistry of the atmosphere, the soil, and the rocks that underlie the habitat). One could draw an imaginary line around any patch of the natural world and regard it as an integrated ecosystem, containing individuals of different species interacting with each other, all being affected by the physical and chemical environment and also modifying that environment by their own presence. A single tree, for example, changes the light intensity, the humidity, and even the chemistry of the space beneath its canopy, affecting what species can grow there.

Certain processes take place within the ecosystem that can be studied only when all of the living and nonliving components of the system are considered together. Energy, for example, is taken into the ecosystem, usually when photosynthetic plants trap the energy of the Sun and use it to convert carbon dioxide gas from the atmosphere into sugars and then other organic molecules. This process is called *primary production* because it represents the first step in the movement of energy into the ecosystem in a form that can be used by organisms in general. Once energy has been trapped in this way the plant can use it to help itself perform work, such as collecting elements from the soil and concentrating them inside its cells. To perform this energy-demanding task, the plant needs to release some of the energy trapped by photosynthesis, and it does this by respiration, a biochemical process that resembles a slow, controlled combustion of the energy-rich sugar within the cells.

The energy that plants bring into the ecosystem fuels not just the plants but also the animals. Animals are unable to fix their own energy from the Sun, so they rely on plants as an energy resource. Herbivores eat the plants; carnivores eat the animals that have eaten the plants. So there are different levels of consumption within the ecosystem, called *trophic levels*. Plants are the first trophic level, herbivores the second, predators that eat herbivores the third, predators that eat other predators the fourth, and so on. Few ecosystems have more than four or five trophic levels. Grass → caterpillar → shrew → kestrel is an example of a *food chain* involving four trophic levels. In fact, energy rarely moves in simple lines through the ecosystem but may pass into a range of tracks, forming a kind of web of different options. This set of relationships is called a *food web* (see "Tundra food webs and energy flow," pages 72–76).

Not all plants and animals are consumed by predators. Some die a natural death or, in the case of plants, various parts—including leaves, stems, flowers, and seeds—may fall to the ground uneaten. The dead remains of organisms provide an energy resource for the decomposers of the ecosystem. These are bacteria and fungi, which, like animals, are unable to fix their own energy but rely on plants for their supplies. Energy from the plants, therefore, can move either into the consumer food web or into the decomposer system. All of these consumers and decomposers, however, use up the energy they acquire as they work and grow. The energy, which is made available through the process of respiration, dissipates in the form of heat as the organisms respire it away. Once energy is trapped by plants it flows through the ecosystem, becoming dissipated and dispersed as it flows.

Chemical elements are also involved in food webs, including the carbon taken by plants from the atmosphere and the nitrogen and phosphorus absorbed by plants from the soil. Plants incorporate these elements into their own structure; nitrogen, for example, is an essential component of all proteins. These elements, too, move through the food webs as one organism consumes another, but, unlike energy, these atoms are not dissipated and lost; they cycle within the ecosystem. When decomposers finally dispose of dead remains, the elements contained are released into the environment, usually the soil, and they are available to plants so that they can be reused and recycled within the ecosystem. Energy flows through the ecosystem from high intensity (sunlight) to low intensity (dissipated heat), while chemical elements cycle within the ecosystem. These two processes, energy flow and nutrient cycling, are fundamental to the functioning of an ecosystem.

The ecosystem concept can be applied at any scale. It is often used when scientists study a particular habitat, such as a pond, an area of woodland, or grassland. But it can be applied at a much smaller scale, perhaps to a decaying log, a clump of grass, or even, in the case of medical studies, to the human gut. Larger units can also be studied using the ecosystem concept, such as a desert, an ocean, or even an entire planet.

## Tundra food webs and energy flow

As in most ecosystems, energy enters the tundra ecosystem in the form of sunlight. The polar tundra is unusual, however, in the way sunlight is distributed over the course of time. In the polar tundra summer, the days become very long and the nights very short. Between the Arctic and Antarctic Circles and the poles there is no night at all for part of the year. In the polar winter, on the other hand, there is little daylight or none at all for part of the time. Day length in alpine tundra varies seasonally according to how far north or south of the equator it is found. Close to the equator there is very little seasonal variation in day length.

The duration of daylight affects the amount of photosynthesis that green plants can achieve. They continue to respire during the hours of darkness, so if day length becomes very short, plants may lose more energy in respiration than they are producing by photosynthesis, in which case they have to draw upon stored food reserves to sustain life. Many plants, therefore, enter a period of dormancy throughout the polar winter so that they can reduce respiration losses of energy to a minimum. Even in alpine tundra, plants may respond to low temperature and snow cover with a winter shutdown rather than try to maintain low levels of productivity.

The short growing season of the tundra ecosystem means that the total amount of primary production (the overall carbon-fixation by green plants) occurring in the course of a year is relatively small compared to that of other ecosystems.

It is not easy to measure primary production accurately for a number of reasons. Some of the energy that accumulates is in the form of roots, and root growth is not easily measured. Parts of plants become detached and decomposed, so ecologists have to make allowances for the losses of litter and the death of roots. Animals, including invertebrates, are constantly consuming plants, so energy is moving along the food webs all the time and is not left to accumulate in the growing plants. Despite all these problems, ecologists have now built up many separate estimates of primary productivity from the various biomes of the world. Generally these estimates are expressed in terms of how much dry weight of plant material accumulates in a specific area of an ecosystem in the course of a year. Dry weights are used because different plants contain different amounts of water, regardless of the amount of energy present. Strictly speaking, it would be better to express productivity data in the form of energy accumulated rather than weight, and sometimes this is done, but weight of plant material is normally used because the variation in energy content of different plant materials is not normally a source of great error.

Tundra vegetation, already described, is very variable (see "Diversity of tundra landscapes," pages 22–23). There are locations where vegetation is unable to survive, and these areas will have no productivity at all. The amount of annual dry matter productivity found within vegetated Arctic tundra habitats ranges from 0.25 to 0.42 pounds per square yard (0.14 to 0.23 $kg/m^2$). Alpine tundra productivity is similar, usually below a value of 0.5 pounds per square yard (0.3 $kg/m^2$). This is very low productivity compared with a tropical rain forest, which has an annual productivity of about 5.4 pounds per square yard (3 $kg/m^2$), or even a temperate deciduous forest yielding 1.8 pounds per square yard (1 $kg/m^2$). It is very similar, however, to the value for annual productivity found in the hot dry deserts of the world. From a productivity point of view, therefore, the tundra ecosystem is equivalent to a desert.

Ecosystems with low primary productivity generally support a limited amount of animal life and have a relatively poor biodiversity, and this is true of the tundra. The diagram

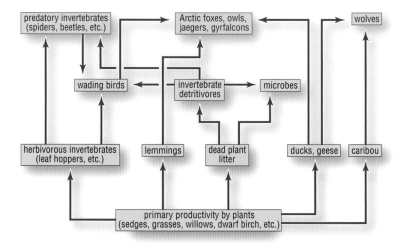

*A food web for a tundra community. All organisms, when they die, provide food for the detritivores and the microbes.*

illustrates the type of food web that is found within tundra ecosystems. New plant material is produced as soon as the light and temperature conditions become favorable in the spring, and invertebrate grazers, including caterpillars, leaf-hoppers, plant-feeding bugs, weevils, and grasshoppers, begin to take advantage of the warm conditions and the availability of fresh food. Predatory invertebrates, including carnivorous beetles, spiders, and harvestmen, then consume the increasing populations of invertebrate grazers. There are also larger animals that take advantage of the growing numbers of insects, including birds. Some birds, such as the rock ptarmigan (*Lagopus mutus*) and willow ptarmigan (*Lagopus lagopus*), are residents in the tundra and feed upon vegetation for most of the year but, in the spring when their young hatch, they also turn to tundra insects as a source of food rich in protein for their growing chicks. Other birds arrive in the Arctic tundra from their winter locations farther south, including a number of wading birds, such as plovers (*Charadrius* species), godwits (*Limosa* species), and sandpipers (*Calidris* species). These take advantage of the long summer days and the rich invertebrate harvest to increase their breeding success. Birds that normally eat seeds, including snow bunting (*Plectrophenax nivalis*), Lapland longspur (*Calcarius lapponicus*), and horned lark (*Eremophila alpestris*), also resort to insectivory at this time of year in the tundra, as they boost their protein intake prior to egg laying.

Ducks and geese arrive in the Arctic tundra as the days lengthen, and they feed directly on vegetation but, like the buntings, also supplement their diet with invertebrate proteins. Caribou (*Rangifer tarandus*) herds move in from the south to their preferred breeding locations and consume the nutrient-rich new growth of vegetation, and small herbivorous mammals, including lemmings (*Clethrionomys* species), take the increased supply of fresh food as a stimulus to begin their breeding cycle.

The increasing numbers of vertebrates provide a food resource for carnivores, including both birds and mammals. Predatory birds, such as gyrfalcons (*Falco rusticolus*), snowy owls (*Nyctaea scandiaca*), and rough-legged hawks (*Buteo lagopus*), hunt their prey over the open tundra. Gyrfalcons feed mainly upon other birds, especially ptarmigan, while the snowy owl and rough-legged hawk concentrate on the small mammals, as do arctic foxes (*Alopex lagopus*). The large grazing mammals, especially caribou, are preyed upon by wolves (*Canis lupus*).

This food web is essentially land-based, but there is also a flow of energy from the marine waters that surround the polar tundra regions. Primary productivity in the oceans is mainly due to the growth of microscopic plants that float in the upper layers of the ocean, called *phytoplankton*. These are food for tiny swimming animals, especially crustaceans, which in turn form the diet of fish and of some of the great whales. Fish are eaten by seals and also by many seabirds, and both of these predatory organisms leave the ocean for breeding and take to the land, either open tundra, cliffs, and beaches or the pack ice. Here, seals may fall prey to one of the top predators of the Arctic tundra, the polar bear (*Ursus maritimus*), and seabirds provide an additional source of food for arctic foxes and predatory birds. One group of birds called *jaegers* (*Stercorarius* species) is not truly predatory, in the sense that they kill their victims, but they do harass fish-catching seabirds and cause them to disgorge their stomach contents, which these food thieves then consume.

Any of these organisms, from the plants to the polar bears, may escape being consumed by an enemy and may die a natural or an accidental death. If this happens, then the dead remains, together with the excreted material of the living animals, enters the soil and is consumed by detritivores and decomposers. Earthworms, the larvae of beetles and crane flies, and tiny springtails all act as detritivores, devouring all kinds of dead material that still contains residual energy and making a living from its breakdown. Finally, the fungi and bacteria in the soil attack whatever remains and extract the last remnants of energy, converting it into heat.

The low primary productivity of the tundra means that only a limited amount of energy enters the ecosystem to support consumers, so food webs tend to be relatively simple compared with those of biomes that have high productivity, such as tropical forests. Food webs also expand and contract according to the season and the availability of energy, so that the winter effectively means a shutdown of the ecosystem. Even the decomposers are unable to remain permanently active because of intense cold. The different living members of the tundra ecosystem either become dormant or leave the area when the winter sets in.

## Nutrient cycling in the tundra

Chemical elements are durable and they can be constantly used and reused by living organisms. The element carbon, for example, which is the most abundant element in living things, is taken out of the atmosphere by photosynthetic plants and is constantly being returned to the atmosphere in the respiration of plants, animals, and microbes. There is an endless cycle of exchange between the living and the nonliving components of the ecosystem. The same is true of all the elements that are found in living bodies.

The atmosphere consists of approximately 80 percent nitrogen gas and 20 percent oxygen. Small traces of other gases are present, the most abundant of which is carbon dioxide, the raw material of photosynthesis, but this composes only about 0.04 percent by volume of the atmosphere, so it is a very tiny component. Most organisms use oxygen for their respiration, and there is no shortage of this material in the atmosphere. Nitrogen is likewise a very important element for all life because it is an essential component of all proteins. But nitrogen gas is highly inert. This means that it is extremely stable and does not easily enter into reactions with other chemicals. So, although the atmosphere is an enormous reservoir of nitrogen, it is effectively unavailable to living things. Fortunately, certain bacteria have developed biochemical techniques for trapping nitrogen gas and converting it into the building blocks of protein. These "nitrogen-fixing" bacteria occur either free-living in the soil or associated with other organisms, such as higher plants (which house them in their roots) or with fungi (which combine with the bacteria to form lichens). The presence of nitrogen-fixing organisms in a community is extremely important because it enables the whole ecosystem to avail itself of the nitrogen reservoir in the atmosphere.

The atmosphere is thus a source of certain vital elements for the sustenance of life. There are two other major reservoirs of chemical elements in ecosystems: One is the soil, and the other is the mass of living things, the biomass.

Soils in tundra regions are formed by the breakdown of underlying rock, so much of their chemical composition is determined by the nature of that rock (see "Soil formation in the tundra," pages 55–57). Many of the rocks underlying the

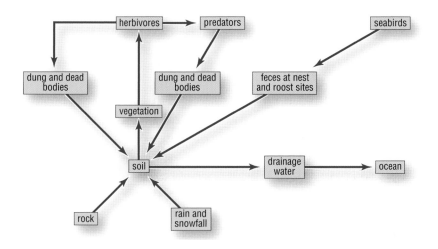

*The cycling of elements in the tundra ecosystem. Nutrients move constantly between soil, vegetation, grazers, and predators. Excretion, death, and decay (conducted by detritivores and decomposers) ensure that elements can be recycled repeatedly.*

*A breeding colony of thick-billed murre* (Uria lomvia) *on a cliff face of the High Arctic island of Spitsbergen, Svalbard. These birds feed on marine fish and then deposit nutrients in their excreta on the tundra landscape at their breeding sites.* (Photo by Patricio Robles Gil/Sierra Madre/Minden Pictures)

polar tundra are poor in chemical elements, but the fact that they are constantly being shattered by freezing and thawing means that there is a constant supply of new material into the soil. The dead remains of plants and animals also serve as a source of elements in the soil. As decomposers extract energy from the organic components of dead material, they also leave behind residual elements, such as nitrogen, phosphorus, calcium, potassium, magnesium, and many others that were once part of the living organism. As they are released, these elements enter the fabric of the soil.

Animals deposit some materials into the soil even before death in their excreta. Urine is a waste product that enables an animal to rid itself of toxic elements and also those materials that are in excess supply, especially nitrogen. Predators, in particular, take in more protein than they need, so their bodies remove the nitrogen component and convert the remainder into carbohydrates or fats. The nitrogen then passes out of the body in the urine. Mammals excrete their nitrogen in the form of urea, while birds and reptiles void it as uric acid, but both provide a source of nitrogen to the soil. Fecal material is more complex because it consists of partially digested organic materials of all kinds. Like urine, however, it is rapidly colonized by soil fungi and bacteria, which liberate many of its component elements and release them into the soil. Some parts of the tundra ecosystem may be strongly influenced by the input of urine and feces, particularly those areas where seabirds roost or breed. In such locations, nutrient elements derived from marine food webs are brought to the land and deposited in great abundance around nests and roosting sites, greatly enhancing the nitrogen and phosphorus content of local soils.

A further source of chemical elements to the soil arrives in the form of rain and snow. As precipitation falls through the atmosphere, it collects dust and other suspended materials, including crystals of salt or droplets derived from the ocean. Precipitation thus brings sodium and chlorine from the sea, together with calcium and magnesium, also present in seawater. In tundra regions lying close to the ocean, the input of these elements can be extremely high, but more isolated and continental areas receive little deposition of this kind. Indeed, as noted previously, the quantity of precipitation over the polar tundra is very low, so nutrient input from this source will also be small (see "Climate in the polar tundra," pages 14–18). Industrial pollution of the atmosphere, however, penetrates far into the uninhabited regions of the world and may bring other chemical elements to the tundra. Radioactive cesium was carried into the tundra regions of northern Europe and Asia following the nuclear accident in the Soviet power station at Chernobyl in 1986. More general in their dispersal are the oxides of nitrogen produced by industrial processes and the combustion of fossil fuels.

Clearly, then, tundra soils can gain nutrient elements in a number of different ways, but these elements can also be lost from soils. Plant roots absorb many of them, expending energy in order to concentrate the required elements from the soil and assemble them into new forms within the plant body. The water that passes through the soil may also take away some of the elements and convey them into neighboring aquatic ecosystems in the process of leaching.

The living bodies of plants and animals form the biomass of the ecosystem, and in most terrestrial ecosystems the vast bulk of the biomass is in the form of vegetation. Vegetation, therefore, represents a major reservoir of chemical elements in most ecosystems. But the tundra does not support bulky vegetation. Even at its most luxuriant, where the ground is clothed in dwarf shrubs of birch and willow, the total amount of dry matter in vegetation does not often exceed one pound per square yard (0.6 kg/m$^2$). This compares with 55 pounds per square yard (30 kg/m$^2$) in a temperate deciduous forest and 75 pounds per square yard (45 kg/m$^2$) in a tropical rain forest. So, although the vegetation of the tundra is an important reservoir of nutrient elements, it is still not a very large one.

The vegetation is grazed by animals, which obtain both energy and chemical elements from this source of food, and these elements pass through the food web in the same patterns as the energy. The main difference is that none of the chemicals are lost to the ecosystem in the process but are recycled through excretion, death, and decay. The decomposers, therefore, play a very important part in the nutrient cycle; if it were not for their activities chemical elements would remain locked up in dead organic matter and would no longer be available for reuse by plants. Decomposition is particularly important in the tundra ecosystem because the total quantity of nutrient elements present is low, so recycling is critical. Decomposition, however, is often limited by two important environmental factors, low temperature and an abundance of soil water.

In well-drained sites during the warmth of the summer, decomposition of organic matter in the soil proceeds rapidly, but in wet sites decomposition is slow because dissolved oxygen is soon consumed. Oxygen diffuses through water 10,000 times more slowly than it does in the atmosphere, so it becomes scarce, and therefore microbial respiration becomes slow under waterlogged conditions. Microbial activity is also affected by low temperature. Just as food lasts longer in a refrigerator, so organic debris remains intact longer in a cold soil, because the microbes fail to break it down. The outcome is that decomposition can be slow at certain times and in some localities in the tundra, leading to the accumulation of organic matter as peat in the soil, and locking some nutrients away from the recycling processes of the ecosystem.

Some ecologists believe that nutrient cycling patterns influence the cycles of population in tundra animals. Population explosions in herbivorous animals, such as lemmings and ptarmigans, could be related to changes in the availability of a vital and limiting element like phosphorus. When phosphorus becomes available as a result of faster decomposition, vegetation grows more rapidly and produces a richer source of nutrition, resulting in faster population growth in the herbivore. This is just one of many suggestions that could account for population cycles in the Arctic.

## Stability of the tundra ecosystem

Some ecosystems are fragile, easily disrupted by disturbance and slow to return to their original condition. A stable ecosystem is one that is not easily perturbed by disruptive forces and can rapidly heal itself if it is damaged. An important question concerning the tundra ecosystem, therefore, is whether it is robust or fragile. Is it a stable ecosystem? There are two ways of measuring stability: First, one can determine how much disturbance must be applied to the ecosystem to unsettle its *inertia*; and second, one can observe how quickly the ecosystem recovers from disturbance (called *resilience*). Most scientists agree that tundra ecosystems are fragile on both counts.

The number of different species of plants, animals, and microbes found in the tundra is relatively low, and ecosystems with few species often lack inertia. The loss of one species as a result of disturbance, such as a pollution episode, could have an impact on many other species, especially any predators that were dependent on the lost species for food. In a more biodiverse ecosystem there would be other species that a predator could turn to, but prey-switching options are limited when the ecosystem is low in diversity.

The soils of the tundra are unstable because of the constant freezing and thawing that they undergo (see "Patterns on the ground," pages 46–53). Soils on slopes are constantly on the move, and any additional pressures on the environment, such as the impact of human trampling or, even worse, the pressure of vehicle wheels, can cause mass instability.

The low biomass and poor nutrient cycling in the tundra ecosystem can also result in fragility. In general, ecosystems with large amounts of biomass (with massive reservoirs of nutrient elements stored in the plant tissues, as in the case of a forest) are less easily disrupted by minor disturbance events than ecosystems with low biomass. It is rather like the world of high finance. A person who has a sum of money to invest in a bank is likely to be concerned about the size of the assets of that bank. If it is a large bank with assets of billions of dollars, then the investment is more likely to be safe than it is in a bank with very limited assets. Similarly with ecosystems: An ecosystem with large nutrient reserves is less likely to become chemically bankrupt than one with small reserves. Tundra ecosystems have very small reserves, so their nutrient capital is always at risk. The fragility of tundra ecosystems is a matter of concern to conservationists (see "Tundra conservation," pages 182–186).

## Conclusions

The tundra can be viewed as an ecosystem because the animals, plants, and microbes that it contains function as an integrated unit, interacting with their chemical and physical setting. Using the ecosystem approach to the study of tundra, it is possible to trace the processes of energy flow and nutrient cycling that link the living and nonliving components of the system.

The energy input from the Sun is relatively low in tundra ecosystems when compared with those of all other biomes, and it is strongly seasonal in its distribution. Polar sites undergo a prolonged winter in which energy input is very low or completely absent. Low temperature in the winter season reduces the primary productivity in both polar and alpine tundra. As a result, energy flow in the tundra ecosystem is limited and consequently there are relatively few links in food chains and food webs. The outcome of these energy limitations is that the number of different types of living organisms that can exist in tundra is restricted.

Nutrient cycling between vegetation and soil is limited by the rate of decomposition, and this is affected by temperature and wetness. Under conditions of low temperature or water-logging there is reduced microbial activity and hence low decomposition. As a result, some elements are locked up in dead organic matter in the ecosystem and are not released for recycling. This slows down the process of nutrient cycling and may restrict plant growth and consequently herbivore abundance.

The low biodiversity, soil instability, and restricted nutrient cycling combine to make the tundra ecosystem relatively fragile. It lacks inertia, so it is easily damaged, and it is not very resilient, so it does not recover quickly from disturbance.

# CHAPTER 4

# BIODIVERSITY OF THE TUNDRA

Life in the tundra is both harsh and bleak. It is not surprising, therefore, that it contains a relatively low diversity of plants, animals, and microbes. Few organisms are able to survive in the difficult conditions that prevail in the tundra, but those that do so are of considerable ecological and evolutionary interest because of their high degree of specialization. Tundra plants and animals have to be tough to endure the problems that face them and they have developed some unusual features that help them to survive.

## Living in the freezer

The cold is the most obvious problem in the tundra. It is not a constant cold; indeed, the temperature in summer on the ground can rise to more than 80°F (26°C), and the high angle of the Sun over tropical mountains can take the daytime temperature well above these levels. But the average temperature is low, and all chemical reactions take place more slowly at low temperatures. This means that the enzymes, the chemicals within all cells that control all operations, are not able to work as fast as they could at higher temperatures. In plants and in animals that are "cold-blooded" (that is, animals that are unable to control their own temperature and simply adopt the temperature of their environment), all activities slow down when the temperature of their surroundings is low. They grow more slowly, they reproduce more slowly, and, in the case of mobile animals, they move more slowly. All of these factors reduce the ability of an organism to compete with its neighbors or to evade attack by a predator. So cold makes the tundra a hard place in which to survive.

In the case of the polar tundra, the habitat is actually dark for a large portion of the year because the Sun never rises.

This is one of the major reasons why average annual temperatures are low, but it provides an additional problem for plants, which depend upon sunlight for the energy needed in photosynthesis. Without light, the green plant is unable to continue its growth. The tundra plant, therefore, must be able to survive in a dormant form in this darkness. Animals that require light to find their food will similarly be disadvantaged by darkness. They can either copy the plants and shut down for the polar winter or adopt the alternative strategy of migrating away from the harsh conditions until things improve in the spring.

Winds can be strong in polar and alpine regions, and they can add to the problems of cold by removing the warm air layers that may cover the surface of an organism. Wind chill further reduces the temperature of both cold-blooded and warm-blooded organisms by stripping these insulating layers. The development of hair on both plants and mammals helps to protect this precious layer of air from being disturbed by the wind. When snow has settled on the ground and has undergone changes by melting and refreezing, it produces small ice particles that can become airborne in the strong winds. The result is that suspended particles of ice are swept along by the moving currents of air, and these have a biting and penetrating impact on any living things, from shrubs to musk oxen. The ice-blasting of these winds can strip away leaves and skin, leaving plants and animals damaged and susceptible to infection.

Burial by snow can be either helpful or harmful. It adds to the effects of darkness, so green plants buried beneath snow patches have a shorter period in summer when they can grow and reproduce. Relatively few plant species are able to cope with this kind of stress, some mosses being among the most tolerant. On the other hand, a snow cover insulates buried organisms from the worst effects of the cold because heat transfer from the ground to the cold air above is slower when there is a snow layer. Hibernating animals and dormant plants are protected from extremely low temperatures and from the impact of ice-blasting while they remain buried.

Drought may also be a problem in polar and alpine tundra habitats. Where the soils are rocky and free draining, water passes quickly through the soil, so plants and any invertebrate animals with low mobility (such as snails and earthworms) can be subjected to desiccation, especially if the rainfall or snowfall is low. In montane areas, precipitation is usually high, but the polar regions have low precipitation and the soil can easily become dry. Tundra plants, therefore, often exhibit adaptations to drought conditions, including evergreen leaves with tough, waxy coverings. The cold can also make water difficult to obtain, especially when it is frozen in the soil. Plants then experience what is known as physiological drought, meaning that there is plenty of water about, but it is in the wrong form or cannot be easily accessed in the soil. Again, the plant is subjected to water stress.

All of these problems add together to make the tundra one of the most difficult environments for plants and animals to live in. The result is that tundra has low overall biodiversity, but the species that do manage to cope are often highly adapted and specialized in their structure and physiology. They are often restricted to the tundra habitat simply because they have become so specialized that they cannot compete with the organisms belonging to any other type of habitat. So the tundra plants and animals represent a distinct group, most of which are found in none of the other biomes of the world. In this way they contribute a very distinctive aspect to the world's biodiversity.

## Tundra plants

The impact of cold and wind blasting has led to the evolution of a distinctive plant life-form in the tundra. Most plants are of a type called *chamaephytes*. These are small shrubs and perennial herbs that grow to a height of just a foot (25 cm) or so and often take the form of a cushion or blanket over the surface of the ground. Thus they hold their buds above the soil surface, yet close to the ground. The advantage of this structure is that the wind moves over the top of the low vegetation. Any shoot that emerges above the general level is damaged and trimmed by the icy blast so the growth is held back. Within the vegetation blanket, the temperature is maintained at a higher level than either above the plant cover in the cold air, or below in the frozen soil of the permafrost. The microhabitat created by this life-form is of great importance to invertebrate animals that can find shelter beneath the plant (and sometimes snow) canopy at the surface of the litter and soil.

Many species of saxifrage provide good examples of cushion-forming chamaephytes. They produce a dense hemisphere of evergreen leaves, and the individual plants often coalesce into hummocky carpets. Beneath the dense surface layer of green leaves is a mass of fibrous stems and dead leaves that provide shelter for a host of invertebrate animals. Dwarf shrubs, such as the arctic heather (*Cassiope tetragona*) and the mountain cranberry (*Vaccinium vitis-idaea*), also form dense hummocks and carpets over the surface of the ground, and even the small Arctic trees, such as the dwarf birch (*Betula nana*) and willows (*Salix* species), rarely raise their heads far above the general canopy.

Just as the aboveground parts of plants do not extend far from the soil surface, so the roots do not penetrate deeply into the ground. Often the soil is poorly structured and rocky (see "Soil types of the tundra," pages 57–61), hindering root penetration, but even where peaty soils provide easier access, the permanently frozen layers prevent deep root development. So most of the activity of roots in the soil, including water absorption and the uptake of nutrient elements, takes place in the uppermost few inches. Root growth begins in the spring as soon as the soil thaws, and continues throughout the growing season. Most of the sideways growth of roots takes place late in the season. These lateral roots allow the plant to forage for nutrients and water in new areas and may also allow the plant to spread.

Protection against drought, either true drought or the physiological variety (that is, lack of water availability because of intense cold), demands certain modifications to plant form. One of the most conspicuous parts of a plant in the tundra is the leaf. Evergreen leaves predominate among tundra plants, so these must provide some advantages in the tundra habitat (see sidebar on page 88). The deciduous habitat is an alternative approach to the problem of survival during drought, for

## Evergreen or deciduous?

Most Arctic and alpine plants are perennial and evergreen. The saxifrages, cranberries, heathers, and willows are all perennial plants. The likely reason for this is that the growing season is so short. As soon as the Sun appears in the spring and the temperature begins to rise, the plants need to start their growth. Being evergreen is an advantage because the leaves that perform the photosynthesis are already present and able to begin their work. Some plants, including the willows and birches, are deciduous, and they need to develop new leaves as soon as conditions improve in the spring. They do this very rapidly but still lag a little behind their evergreen competitors. Where they gain some advantage is in their smaller bulk during the harsh winter. Stems without leaves are less likely to be damaged by wind blasting than those that still bear a leafy cover. So there is a kind of trade-off between keeping leaves through the winter and losing them, each strategy having certain advantages and disadvantages. On the whole, however, the evergreen habitat probably proves the more effective and successful. Evergreen leaves have one additional advantage: Constructing them costs less. When a plant builds a new leaf it has to invest some of its food reserves, including the sugars produced by photosynthesis and the nutrient elements, such as nitrogen, phosphorus, and potassium, taken out of the soil by the roots. Evergreen leaves last longer, perhaps two or three years, so the investment is more worthwhile.

the presence of fewer leaves during fall and winter means that the plant requires less in the way of water supply. This is one of the great advantages of being deciduous. Evergreen leaves could result in water loss to the plant through the whole year, so they need to be constructed in such a way that water loss is reduced to a minimum. The long-lasting evergreen leaves are usually thick, rounded, and glossy with wax, and they may bear a cover of hairs. All of these adaptations serve to reduce water loss by cutting down the evaporation of water (transpiration) from the pores upon the leaf surfaces. In addition to reducing water loss, some of these adaptations, such as silvery hairs on the leaf surface, can also serve to reflect light and to prevent the leaf from becoming heated. If a leaf becomes hot it loses water faster, so keeping the leaf cool on a hot summer day can be important even in the tundra.

One method some plants adopt in order to avoid periods of great stress is to die. It sounds like an extreme solution to the problem, but the plant may leave behind a reserve of seeds in the soil that can germinate when conditions are more favorable once more. Annual plants of this kind, however, are extremely rare in the tundra. One annual plant that has proved successful is the Iceland purslane (*Koenigia islandica*). This exceptional little plant, only two inches (5 cm) high, is found in the Arctic and subarctic, in the mountains of Asia and the Rocky Mountains of North America, and on the southern tip of South America, in Tierra del Fuego. So it is clearly a very successful plant of tundra habitats despite being an annual. The problem with being an annual plant is that the entire life cycle (germination, establishment, growth, flowering, and fruiting) has to take place in a single growing season. Where the season is very short (as in the tundra) this can be extremely difficult, so annuals are rare. But where there is perpetual daylight, a very fast-developing annual can make it, and the Iceland purslane fits this bill. It grows in open rocky areas and at the end of the summer season it dies completely, leaving only its tiny seeds in the surface layers of soil. These survive the rigors of winter beneath a blanket of snow and begin the cycle again the following spring.

A feature of Arctic and alpine plants that has made them extremely attractive to gardeners is that they often bear very large flowers in comparison to their small stature. The purple saxifrage (*Saxifraga oppositifolia*), for example, is a tiny cushion plant that has large purple flowers, and these flowers are larger in the most northern populations of the Arctic than they are in more southerly regions. The brilliant blue gentians (*Gentiana* species) of the European Alps and some poppies, such as the arctic poppy (*Papaver radicatum*), have extremely large and showy flowers. Since the general tendency of tundra plants is to maintain a low profile, it may seem strange that they often have such conspicuous flowers. The reason is probably their need to attract insect pollinators in an environment where time is short and competition for the limited number of appropriate insects is high. Flowers are a kind of advertisement that demands the attention of passing insects and, like the billboards along a highway, each flower is trying to outcompete its neighbors in visual attraction. In such situations

*The spring gentian (Gentiana verna), growing on the mountains of Switzerland, blooms as soon as the winter snow has melted. As with many alpine plants, its flowers are large and brightly colored in order to attract the attention of pollinating insects.* (Photo by Peter D. Moore)

large flowers with bright colors are likely to succeed best. Some flowers may even turn during the course of the day, always facing the Sun. In this way they gather heat, which further encourages insect activity (see sidebar on opposite page).

The high mountains of the Tropics are a home to some remarkable plants. Many of the typical Arctic-alpine plant species of the high latitudes have failed to colonize these isolated patches of tundra habitat, far from the main regions of the tundra biome. The outcome is that some types of plants that are not usually associated with tundra have evolved some features that enable them to survive in the cold conditions that they find there. Among these are members of the genera *Senecio* (a group that includes the ragwort) and *Lobelia* (a group that includes the cardinal flower and Indian tobacco). Both of these plant groups are generally herbaceous (that is, they have no woody tissue) but in the tropical tundra habitats they have taken on a most remarkable form (see illustration above). They

# Solar-tracking flowers

The flowers of many tundra plants have the capacity to track the Sun across the sky. Often their petals have the curved shape of parabolic reflectors that can gather sunlight and focus it upon the vital part of the flower, the fruit-producing carpels. In this way they can ensure that the development of their reproductive structures gains as much energy as possible. But the energy-focusing effect of the petals is also a means of making life easier for the pollinators. Most pollinators in the tundra are cold-blooded insects, whose activity is determined by their immediate energy intake, often largely from the Sun. So providing the insects with a hot flower ensures that they can work faster and provide a more effi- cient pollination. Poppies are an excellent example of this use of flower shape to encour- age visits from cold pollinators. The visual outcome of the flower's need to attract pollinators is that many tundra habitats, especially the high mountains, are decorated by a wide variety of large and colorful flowers through the summer season.

*In the cold alpine climate some flowers, such as this alpine pasque flower* (Pulsatilla alpina) *in Switzerland, track the Sun across the sky and gather warmth by adopting a parabolic shape that focuses the rays on the flower's center.* (Photo by Peter D. Moore)

*The alpine zone of high mountains in equatorial regions is home to some remarkable plants. Giant senecios, such as the species* Senecio elgonensis *shown here on Mount Elgon, Uganda, East Africa, are treelike forms of a plant group that is normally herbaceous.* (Photo by Peter D. Moore)

produce thick, treelike trunks that are clothed with a compact mass of dead leaf bases that wrap around the trunks like fur coats. Like animal fur, this fibrous covering forms an insulating layer around the living cells of the stem. Although frost damage is a problem that plants of the Tropics do not normally face, at night the air temperature at 13,000 feet (3,800 m) can fall below freezing even on the equator. The layer of leaf bases on the trunks of the giant *Senecio* and *Lobelia* plants ensure that even if the air temperature falls to 25°F (–4°C), the temperature beneath the insulating layer, where the living cells are found, remains at about 36°F (2°C). For a tropical plant, this is the difference between life and death.

Coping with the cold is evidently the most serious problem for tundra plants. Unlike mammals that can migrate or hibernate beneath the snow and maintain a living body temperature by their biochemical activities, plants (together with microbes and cold-blooded animals) assume the temperature of their surroundings, and this can be very low. That is why many are clothed in wrappings of dead leaves or high densities of hair. The real problem for living cells when they are exposed to intense cold is that their high water content puts them in danger of freezing. If an automobile is left out in severe cold without the protection of antifreeze compounds in its cooling system, then the water in its radiator and pipes will freeze. The driver may not notice this until the thaw comes, and then it becomes obvious that the pipes have burst because all the water leaks out. The problem is, of course, that water expands when it freezes and thus ruptures the pipes, but this becomes evident only when the temperature rises. It is the same with plants. The freezing of a cell involves ice crystals forming inside the cell itself, and the frozen water occupies a greater volume, so it may begin to damage the structure of the cell, particularly the membranes that surround the delicate organelles within the cell (nucleus, chloroplasts, mitochondria, and so on). When the thaw comes, the damage becomes evident and the ruptured membranes often lead to the death of the cell.

Just as people use antifreeze to prevent damage to their cars, plants have developed antifreeze compounds that can help them cope with low temperature. Most chemicals, when dissolved in water, lower its freezing point, acting as a sort of antifreeze. Common salt, for example, is used in this way on highways to reduce the impact of frost. This explains why the sea freezes only when the temperature is well below that needed to freeze freshwater. But salt is not a good material to use as antifreeze either in automobiles or in living cells. It is corrosive in the metal tubes of an engine, and it causes damage to enzymes in a cell. In the cell, it can be accumulated in the vacuole, which is a kind of reservoir carefully enclosed and separated from the working parts of the cell by a membrane, but it cannot be used in the cytoplasm, the living and working part of the cell. Other compounds, however, can be used, such as certain amino acids, which are the component units of proteins. The amino acid proline, for example, serves as antifreeze in some plants as well as in some fish. Additionally, some plants use sugars and sugar alcohols, such as glycerol, mannitol, and sorbitol. In these ways, plants can lower the freezing point of their cell contents and increase their chances of survival.

Among the plants that cope best in tundra habitats are the mosses. This may seem surprising, but despite their small stature and delicate structure, mosses are actually very tough. They have no waxy covering to prevent their leaves from desiccating, but many species are able to survive in a dry state for years without losing their ability to recover and grow once again. They can also continue to photosynthesize and grow at lower temperatures than is possible for most flowering plants. The moss *Bryum argenteum,* for example, can continue to photosynthesize below the freezing point of water. The success of the mosses in tundra habitats can be judged by the fact that the whole of Antarctica contains only two species of flowering plants but more than 100 species of mosses. Biologists often refer to mosses as being "primitive" in the sense that they are structurally simple and have a low position on the evolutionary scale, but this does not mean that they are unable to compete with more advanced plants when conditions are tough.

## Microbes of the tundra

When people want to preserve foodstuffs over long periods, they store them in a refrigerator or, better still, in a freezer. This is to prevent bacteria and fungi consuming the food. Just like humans and other animals, most bacteria and all fungi obtain the energy they need for life from organic materials that have ultimately been assembled by green plants. If food lies unattended in warm temperatures, then microbes (bacteria and fungi) soon make use of it and, from the human point of view, it decomposes. When people are cunning enough to put food in very cold containers, most bacteria and fungi are unable to attack it because their biochemistry, like humans', is adapted to operate in warmer temperatures. For much of the year, the tundra is like a gigantic freezer, and almost all microbial activity ceases. But in the summer, the soil, where most of the microbes live, becomes warmer, the water within it melts, and the microbes take up their activity once more.

There is plenty of food for microbes in many tundra soils. When the spring comes, the soil is usually rich in dead plant material derived from the previous year's growth, or even from before that. Some of the organic materials in tundra soils may date back many thousands of years and yet still lie only partially decomposed. This is why the remains of humans buried in the tundra during early expeditions of discovery have remained intact and have occasionally been recovered by more recent travelers. It is why the remains of mammoths are still being recovered from the Siberian tundra; Russian restaurants have even been known to serve mammoth steaks. So the microbes are well supplied with food, but the physical conditions of the winter prove too severe for most of the bacteria and fungi found in temperate, warmer soils, and only very few species are present to begin their spring activities. The microbial biodiversity of the tundra, in other words, is very low when compared with that of warmer climates. But those microbes that are present perform very valuable tasks, enabling nutrients to cycle so that they are not locked up permanently in dead matter, and fixing nitrogen from the atmosphere, which is so vital to both the plants and animals of the tundra (see "Nutrient cycling in the tundra," pages 76–81).

Very little is known about how the cold-loving microbes manage to function at low temperature. Some, of course, survive the extreme cold as resistant spores and thus avoid being desiccated or having their cell membranes ruptured by the formation of ice crystals. Others may avoid the problem completely by becoming extinct in a site each winter and then invading again by aerial dispersal every spring. The very small size of the dustlike spores and their capacity for long-distance movements in the air would easily allow such reinvasion every year. But some microbes do manage to maintain activity even at very low temperatures, and these probably survive the tundra winter. The enzymes (proteins in the cells that manage most of the cell processes) of these cold-loving microbes must be able to function at low temperature and avoid the molecular breakdown that would occur in most plant and animal cells under those conditions. Microbes use antifreeze compounds in a similar way to some tundra plants. They may accumulate sugars, or glycerol, or various fats in their cells that lower their freezing point, and in this way they can remain unfrozen even at temperatures of 5°F (–15°C). Understanding how microbes operate at low temperature might enable scientists to use genetic manipulation to construct plants and animal that would similarly grow and function under low temperature. There could be opportunities here for developing a cold-climate agriculture that would help to feed the world. Such an understanding could also be of great importance in the food storage industry in trying to prevent the destruction of frozen foods by certain microbes and thus increasing the storage life of foods.

One very important group of microbes in the tundra is the blue-green bacteria (often referred to as blue-green algae, which is not strictly accurate). As their name implies, these are pigmented (colored) microbes, and they use their pigments to catch the energy of sunlight and to fix carbon dioxide in photosynthesis. They therefore contribute to the energy-fixing process in the tundra community. Because of this, just like green plants, they are able to live only in locations that receive light. They are found mainly on the surface of the soil, or in association with fungi in the lichens on the rocks or on the ground. Not only do they create organic matter from inorganic carbon by photosynthesis, they are also capable of taking nitrogen from the atmosphere and incorporating it into organic molecules, including proteins, so that it then becomes available to plants and animals. The blue-green bacteria, therefore, play a vital role in the functioning of the tundra ecosystem. Some blue-green bacteria associate with fungi in the formation of lichens (see sidebar on opposite page), which are also important components of many tundra communities.

Lichens, judging by their abundance, clearly have great advantages in the tundra habitat. They contain photosynthetic organisms (the algae or the blue-green bacteria), so they need light to supply the energy they require. They also have a fungal component, and the function the fungus serves is to provide a protective structure in which the photosynthetic component can operate. So, most of the crusty, leafy, or branched parts of the thallus (the body of the lichen) are composed of fungal tissue. A close look under a microscope shows that the fungus consists of a mass of interweaving strands, forming a spongy tissue, within which the green cells of their associated species are located. The spongy fungal tissue is highly efficient as protection against the elements, particularly against the impact of frost and drought, the two chief problems that face isolated algal cells in the

## Lichens

Lichens are both abundant and very apparent in the tundra regions. The lichen is a remarkable construction that looks like a single organism (and is classified and named as such by biologists) but is in fact a combination of two separate organisms, closely bound in an interdependent union. The combination consists of a fungus and either a green alga or a blue-green bacterium.

The body of the lichen (the thallus) can take on a variety of forms. It may form a crust, almost like paint, on the surface of a rock, or it may take on a leaflike form, curling up at the edges, or it may even have stalklike structures that stand up from the ground and may branch like miniature trees. Even the tallest of lichens, however, are rarely more than two inches (5 cm) in height. But since they can grow in dense colonies and can form compact mats over the surface of the ground (especially over shallow and dry soils), they may form the main vegetation cover in some of the polar semidesert regions of the tundra. Where there is taller vegetation, such as dwarf shrubs, lichens may grow on the surface of the shoots and branches of their hosts. When they adopt this way of life, they do not act as parasites but simply use their host as a means of support and of escape from the shade on the ground beneath. An organism that uses a plant for support in this way is called an epiphyte. Epiphytism is a very common way of life in tropical rain forests, where obtaining light can be a severe problem, but it is found even in the tundra habitat if shrubs are present.

tundra. The alga (or blue-green bacterium) thus provides the food by photosynthesis, and the fungus provides the protection in return for a share of the food. If the photosynthetic component is a blue-green bacterium, then the lichen is also a means of nitrogen fixation, so this is a source of nutrition for many other tundra organisms.

Many lichens are strongly pigmented and have bright colors; orange is particularly common. The pigments protect the delicate cells from the high intensity of light, especially ultraviolet radiation, in the clear air of the tundra. One disadvantage of lichens is that they are very slow growing, so they are sensitive to high levels of grazing (by animals such as caribou) and to trampling that can crush and damage their branching structures. Despite their sensitivity to physical damage, lichens are tough under cold conditions, as illustrated by their ability to continue photosynthesis in very low temperatures. The lichen *Umbilicaria aprina,* for example, is still photosynthetically active at 2°F (–17°C). So lichens exceed even the mosses when it comes to coping with the cold.

Although microbial biodiversity in the tundra is low, the value of these organisms for ecosystem function can be very high. People often evaluate habitats according to their biodiversity. Tropical rain forests and coral reefs are held in high regard, for example, because they are so diverse, and this is reasonable. But the tundra is valuable despite its low biodiversity because it contains such remarkably well adapted species; they are packets of genes that are found nowhere else on Earth.

## Tundra invertebrates

Invertebrate animals (animals without backbones) are extremely numerous in almost all the habitats of the world, and the tundra is no exception. All invertebrates, however, have the disadvantage of being cold-blooded, which means that their body temperature is largely determined by the temperature of their surroundings. In a cold habitat, such as the tundra, this limits the activities that invertebrate animals can undertake, especially during the winter season. Invertebrates are generally much smaller than vertebrates, so it is useful to try to see a habitat from an invertebrate's point of view. For an animal the size of an ant, the mat of lichens and mosses on the surface of the soil appears as a forest would appear to a person, having a high canopy and branches and a sheltered floor beneath that lies in its shade. Within this microhabitat, therefore, the conditions may be very different from those in the air up above. The temperature will fluctuate less, because the trapped air layer beneath the canopy neither heats up so much in the day nor cools down so rapidly at night. The humidity also remains high, which is an important consideration for many invertebrates that lose water easily through their body surfaces.

The soil itself is also an important habitat for invertebrates within the tundra, for the surface layers are usually warm and moist during the summer months. Many different types of invertebrates manage to make a living here. There are two types of worm, for example, the nematodes (phylum Nematoda) and the enchytraeids (phylum Annelida). Nematodes are among the most numerous and diverse of all animal groups. In tundra soils as many as 5 million have been recorded within 1.2 square yards (1 m$^2$). They have bodies that are not divided into segments and they have a very wide range of lifestyles. Most are detritivores, which means that they feed upon dead organic matter, mainly derived from the fallen litter of plants. Some feed upon algae in the soil, or even on soil bacteria. But there are others that prey on other small invertebrates or are parasites upon larger animals, including mammals, or on higher plants. Some eat fungi, including lichens, but there are some fungi that reverse the feeding chain and trap nematodes in ringlike snares, thus killing them and feeding upon their decaying remains. Some nematodes are highly tolerant of low temperature. The nematode worm *Panagrolaimus davidi,* for example, remains unfrozen even at a temperature of –40°F (–40°C) because of the antifreeze chemicals in its body. The enchytraeid worms are also largely detritivores, but they differ in having bodies that are divided into segments, rather like the common earthworm but very much smaller. They are particularly abundant in organic, peaty soils.

The springtails (Collembola) are another group of detritivorous invertebrates. These are tiny, wingless insects that gain their name from a forked spine at the rear of their bodies that can flick outward, allowing the animal to spring into the air. This usually occurs when they are disturbed, so this trick presumably functions as a means of escaping a predator. The fact that springtails cannot fly raises the question of how these small creatures are so widely dispersed in the Arctic, often on isolated islands. Recent studies have shown that they are capable of surviving for long periods on the surface of the sea and can be dispersed in this way. Their bodies are covered with very small hairs and scales that make them virtually incapable of becoming wet, so they float on the water surface instead of sinking. This can be observed when water is added to a potted plant, because springtails are usually present in the soil and they often float on the surface of the water that has been added. So springtails can disperse on ocean surfaces to distant islands and coasts; mountain populations of springtails with an Arctic distribution, however, are more difficult to account for. It is likely that these were left behind after the last ice age. One species of springtail, *Tetracanthella arctica,* is found in Greenland and Iceland and also in the Pyrenees Mountains of Spain and France. It is unlikely that it spread from the Arctic islands to the continental mountains, but perhaps it was once much more widely distributed and, as the ice retreated and forests spread, this cold-loving species of springtail became confined to the isolated peaks and the high-latitude islands.

The tundra contains many wetland habitats, including pools and peaty mires (see "Diversity of tundra landscapes," pages 22–23). These are rich areas for many invertebrates, including midge and mosquito larvae (both in the order Diptera). Some of the midge larvae, such as the chironomids (family Chironomidae), can also live in soils. Any human visitor to the tundra in summer is bound to be impressed by the abundance of biting insects; clouds of mosquitoes arise whenever vegetation in the wet tundra is disturbed. Only the female mosquito takes blood, and she requires this in order to lay her eggs and complete her life cycle. Fortunately, the species of mosquito found in the tundra do not convey any parasitic diseases, unlike their tropical relatives, but their bites can be extremely irritating and can cause blisters and inflammation. Although people tend not to appreciate this abundance of insect life in the Arctic, many birds do. Several bird species move into the tundra to exploit this source of food during their summer breeding seasons (see "Tundra birds," pages 102–111).

Plant-feeding insects are found in the tundra, including some beetles (especially weevils; family Curculionidae) and also the crane flies (family Tipulidae). Some plant-eating insects, such as the sawflies (suborder Symphyta), lay their eggs in the leaves of dwarf willows, and as the larva develops, the leaves produce extra tissues, forming grotesque swellings, or galls. Eventually the mature insect emerges from these, mates, and goes on to lay eggs in new leaves. Many flies and butterflies serve important functions as pollinators for the flowering plants, and they obtain their food from the supplies of nectar or surplus pollen from these plants. There are also surprisingly many moths that continue the pollination process during the tundra night. One of the most spectacular butterflies of the alpine tundra is the Apollo (*Parnassus apollo*). It is a European species but is a member of a group of butterflies found in North America, Europe, and Asia, into the Himalayas. Black and white in color, it has large spots on its hind wings that look like eyes, and these serve to distract a predator when they are suddenly flashed as the insect opens its wings. Both the wings and the body of the Apollo are densely hairy, and this is a feature of the butterflies of alpine and Arctic habitats, helping to conserve warmth. The large wings provide the Apollo with strong flight and the ability to soar rather than flutter. These qualities are very advantageous in the mountains, where winds are often strong and flight for a light organism, such as a butterfly, is risky. Indeed, many insects in the mountains have lost the ability to fly as flight can be a source of danger rather than an aid to dispersal.

Another butterfly family that has proved successful in both Arctic and alpine habitats is the Satyridae, which includes meadow browns and wood nymphs, found both in the Old World and the New World. These butterflies are good examples of the predominance of dark colors in the tundra insects. While this seems to go against the trend found in the birds and mammals, which are often white or pale colored for camouflage, it must be remembered that butterflies are active only in the summer period, when snow is less abundant and both the ground and the vegetation are dark. Also, dark colors are more effective at absorbing heat from the Sun, and in a cold-blooded animal this is an important source of energy. The generally small size of tundra insects may also be related to energy transfer (see sidebar on page 102). A small insect has a larger amount of surface per unit of body size, so if it basks in the sunshine it can quickly transfer heat to all its parts. Mammals, on the other hand, have evolved very different strategies. Because they are warm-blooded it is heat loss that concerns them, not heat gain, so a small surface area per unit volume is preferable and most mammals of the tundra are large and relatively rounded in shape (see "Alpine tundra mammals," pages 121–126).

Once an adult insect emerges in the spring, the process of locating a member of the opposite sex, mating, and egg laying becomes urgent, and some insects have developed a shortcut for avoiding the risks involved in the mating process. Blackflies, many midges, stone flies, and sucking

## Energy and tundra insects

Energy is the controlling concern of tundra insects. Even the flies that are responsible for the consumption of dead bodies of birds and mammals lay their eggs first on the side of the carcass that faces the Sun, for the larvae develop faster within the heated meat. Butterflies and flies bask wherever they find a combination of sunshine and shelter from the wind. Within the cups of flowers facing the Sun is a favorite location. Of all the insects, only some bumblebees have mastered the art of generating a little heat of their own. They vibrate their wings violently, causing an intense buzzing noise and building up heat by friction. Some flowers have developed a mechanism of pollen release that relates to this frantic buzzing, the pollen-bearing anthers rupturing in response to the resonant vibration created by the bee and showering it with pollen.

Although insects have adapted to take advantage of any opportunity to obtain solar energy in the tundra, the predominant temperature is low. For this reason many of the processes of growth and development have to take place in the cold. In the case of mosquito larvae, for example, growth and development from egg to adult can take place in temperatures just above freezing point. Even so, development is slow and many insects may take two years to complete their growth and reproductive cycle instead of the usual one. The larvae must therefore develop mechanisms for survival through the winter, which involve the use of antifreeze chemicals and sometimes the desiccation of their bodies into a torpid, dormant state.

bugs have virtually abandoned sexual reproduction. Males are extremely rare or absent, and the females lay eggs requiring no fertilization. This is obviously a simpler and faster reproductive system, similar to the vegetative propagation of plants. But it has the disadvantage that the offspring are all clones of the parent, so new variations are not being introduced into the population. There is a trade-off between genetic diversity and speed of replication, and the system could misfire if there are sudden changes in the environment, such as climate change.

## Tundra birds

The long days and the abundant supplies of insects and berries, together with the availability of seafood along the coasts, make the Arctic a very attractive place for migrant birds to breed. The Antarctic also has an abundance of marine food resources, but the generally poor vegetation limits its possibilities for birds that do not depend on the ocean. Mountain tundra also provides local food supplies from alpine vegetation, but it generally lacks the oceanic advantages and certainly cannot supply the long daylight hours for feeding the young, unless the mountains happen to lie within the Arctic Circle. So the tundra, especially the Arctic tundra, attracts immigrant bird populations during the summer months. Alaska has 113 species of breeding birds, while the Canadian Arctic has 105 species and the Russian Arctic 136. These are quite high numbers considering how far north these regions lie. But very few of these bird species remain in the Arctic through the winter.

The willow ptarmigan (*Lagopus lagopus*) and the rock ptarmigan (*Lagopus mutus*) are good examples of the truly Arctic residents. These two birds are found right around the Arctic and subarctic regions of the world and are difficult to distinguish from each other. Both are almost pure white in winter, with just a little dark on the tail, while in summer they become dark brown with only the wings remaining white. They flock together during the winter and split into pairs for the breeding season in summer. As their names imply, they have different habitat preferences, the willow ptarmigan preferring dwarf shrub tundra while the rock ptarmigan occupies mainly the open rocky regions with little vegetation cover. Apart from their change in color with season, which has a clear advantage for avoiding predators, they also have feathered feet, which prevents heat loss to the snow and the cold ground. Both species are mainly plant eaters, consuming the young growth of leaves, together with berries; they also eat insects during the spring. The tundra's abundant insect supply is important in providing protein for the young birds in the nest.

Other permanent residents of the Arctic are the snowy owl (*Nyctea scandiaca*), the peregrine falcon (*Falco peregrinus*), and the gyrfalcon (*Falco rusticolus*), all of them predators. The gyrfalcon is a large falcon that preys mainly upon the two ptarmigan species (88 percent of the diet in Alaska and 96 percent in Greenland consists of ptarmigans). Other prey animals include seabirds, snow bunting (*Plectrophenax nivalis*), and small mammals, such as lemmings (*Dicrostonyx* species). The somewhat smaller peregrine falcon competes with the gyrfalcon for ptarmigan in the Arctic. The peregrine falcon is much more widely distributed throughout the Northern Hemisphere, but it succeeds well in the tundra regions, nesting on cliffs. Snowy owls are also important predators of the tundra, but their main food source is the lemming. Like the lemming's, the snowy owl's population fluctuates strongly depending upon the availability of its prey. White-tailed eagles (*Haliäetus albicilla*) are often associated with tundra coasts, as in western Greenland, but these are mainly fish-feeders and only occasionally take tundra birds and mammals, such as the arctic fox (*Alopex lagopus*).

Among the smaller, perching birds, the hoary redpoll (*Carduelis hornemanni*) is one of the most truly tundra species, being resident in much of the Arctic region, although in winter it tends to move southward into southern Canada, so it should really be regarded as a partial migrant. The common redpoll (*Carduelis flammea*) is mainly a summer visitor to the tundra, preferring the shrub tundra and willow thickets to the open tundra landscapes. Both are mainly seed eaters. Several other perching birds visit the tundra to breed and then move south for the winter. The Lapland longspur (*Calcarius lapponicus*) is one such bird that breeds on the open short grass habitats in the tundra of Canada and Alaska and moves south into the United States for the winter. It is also found in the Eurasian tundra and again migrates into the temperate zone around the Black and Caspian Seas to avoid the severity of the tundra winter. The Lapland longspur is mainly brown in coloration, the male having a black facial mask and yellow beak in summer. Some of the tundra perching birds use white patches and wings as a means of camouflage in sites that retain some summer snow. The snow bunting (*Plectrophenax nivalis*), for example, has a brown body and white wings with black tips. When it flies among rocks and snow patches it becomes very conspicuous, but it seems to disappear once it lands and closes its wings. A predator trying to locate it would be greatly confused by the way it appears and then vanishes so effectively. Snow buntings, like Lapland longspurs, breed on barren, open ground in the polar tundra, but their range extends south in Europe on the Scandinavian and Scottish mountains. In North America they come south only in the winter. They are mainly seed eaters and they carry seeds in their crops when they migrate. When a new volcanic island arose out of the sea off the coast of Iceland, some of the first land plants to arrive came in the guts of migrating snow buntings. Some of these birds made a landfall and then died, but their crops still contained living seeds that they had eaten, possibly as far away as Scotland, and these germinated within the birds' corpses and formed the first wave of land plant invasion on the island.

The snow bunting does not occur on more southerly mountains except as a winter visitor in North America, but the mountains of Europe and Asia have a very similar bird called the snowfinch (*Montifringilla nivalis*) that spends its entire life on the alpine tundra, changing its altitudinal range a little with seasons. It occurs in the Pyrenees, Alps, Caucasus, and eastward into the mountains of Tibet and China. It is very like the snow bunting in appearance, with its black-tipped white wings, and uses the same tricks to evade predators, but it is not very closely related. This is a good example of how evolution can come up with the same answer to a challenge on more than one occasion.

Many types of waterbirds spend their summers in the Arctic and breed there in the peace and tranquility, far from human settlements. These include wading birds and also ducks and geese. Some of the most familiar waders of North American winter coasts, such as the red knot (*Calidris canutus*), the sanderling (*Calidris alba*), and the dunlin (*Calidris alpina*), breed in the very far north of the Arctic and migrate over huge distances to do so, despite their diminutive size. They find the tundra ideal for their breeding as there is an abundant supply of aquatic invertebrates in the tundra wetlands. Most of these waders, as their name implies, have long legs in relation to their bodies so that they can wade into shallow, muddy pools and probe the mud with their long bills. Some of them, like the phalaropes (*Phalaropus* species), have developed a behavior pattern in which they swim rapidly in circles. This creates a vortex in the water that brings the mud and the

## *Putting on weight in the tundra*

Wading birds, like all migrants, need to accumulate large reserves of fat in their bodies to supply the energy needed for the long migration flight. The sanderling, for instance, doubles its weight just prior to the migration and loses all of this excess of fat during the strenuous journey. Some wading birds spend the winter in the southern parts of South America and Africa. Most of the journey is carried out at night, using the stars to assist in navigation, together with the kind of magnetic compass that birds have within their brains and that enables them to find a correct course even in cloudy weather. During the day they rest at stopover sites where they can replenish their food supplies. In the case of waders, many migrate along coastlines so that suitable habitats are quite frequent, but some pass over the land, even over deserts, where isolated water sources become vital for their successful completion of the journey.

small animals it contains to the surface, where the phalarope can feed upon them. Their chicks are said to be *nidifugous,* which means that they can walk and run within an hour of hatching, and they leave the nest to shelter in the long vegetation of cotton grasses and sedges. Their parents continue feeding them through the long summer days, but they quickly develop the ability to feed themselves and prepare for the long journey that lies ahead of them. Storing enough energy in the form of fat is vital if migrant birds are to complete their long journeys successfully (see sidebar above).

Ducks, geese, and swans—the waterfowl—also find an ideal breeding ground in the Arctic tundra. The small, dark brant goose (*Branta bernicla*), for example, breeds on the tundra throughout the northern fringe of North America and Greenland, and a closely related species breeds in northern Russia. Like the waders, it tends to migrate along the coasts and spends its winter in estuaries and coastal areas farther south, even as far as Florida and Baja California. The snow goose (*Chen caerulescens*), on the other hand, which also breeds in Arctic Canada and Alaska, has several inland flyways: west down the Sierras, through central North America along the Mississippi River, and also down to the East Coast, cutting through Hudson Bay and Ontario. These flyways are also used by the white-fronted goose (*Anser albifrons*). This species is more widespread than the snow goose, however, being found in western Greenland and through northern Russia and Siberia. There are several subspecies of this goose, each of which has its own breeding area, migration route, and winter habitat, as shown in the illustration. The Greenland population, for example, travels to Ireland and western Britain to spend the winter. These separate populations have probably established their flyway behavior patterns since the end of the last glaciation. The separation of these different groups of birds with their various patterns of movement has ensured that they have begun to evolve separately. Many different species of waterfowl use the same flyways, including the aptly named tundra swan (*Cygnus columbianus*), which travels to the Gulf of Mexico and other coastal regions for the winter. This same swan breeds in the Russian tundra and travels all the way to England in the west or to Japan in the east for its winter season.

Seabirds are a feature of the tundra coastlines and use both the flat, open tundra and the cliffs of the more mountainous locations for their breeding. Some of them, such as Ross's gull (*Rhodostethia rosea*) and the ivory gull (*Pagophila eburnean*), spend virtually all their lives in the cold northern oceans and the fringing land, but others breed in the tundra and then migrate to more southern coasts for the winter. These migrants include eider ducks (genera *Somateria* and *Polystica*) and long-tailed ducks (*Clangula hyemalis*), the common murre (*Uria aalge*) and the pigeon guillemot (*Cepphus columba*) of the west coast of North America and the razorbill

*The breeding range, wintering grounds, and migration routes of the white-fronted goose.*

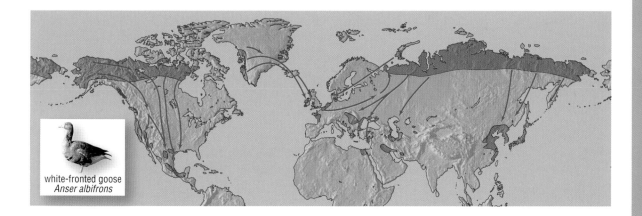

white-fronted goose
*Anser albifrons*

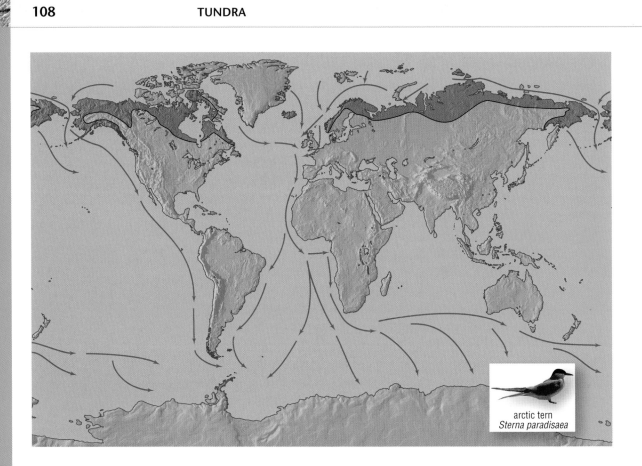

*The breeding range and the migration routes of the arctic tern* (Sterna paradisea), *perhaps the best-traveled of all birds*

arctic tern
*Sterna paradisaea*

(*Alca torda*) of the east coast. The Pacific loon (*Gavia pacifica*) is another seagoing migrant that moves along the west coast in flocks of several hundred as it migrates between the tundra and the ocean off Mexico, where it spends the winter. But of all the migrant seabirds that nest in the tundra the prize for the most well traveled must go to the arctic tern (*Sterna paradisaea*). This small white bird, sometimes called a "sea swallow" because of its elegant flight and long forked tail, breeds throughout the tundra regions of the north. It then sets off on a journey that takes it deep into the Southern Hemisphere, all the way to Antarctica and the Southern Ocean (see illustration above). Researchers have studied its main migration routes by banding birds (placing small, harmless rings marked with code numbers around their legs) and recording their places of recovery when they are trapped for observation or found dead. The arctic terns from North America and eastern Russia move from the Arctic mainly down the west coast of America (North, Central, and South), while those from Greenland, Europe, and western Russia travel down the west coast of Europe and Africa. They then disperse in the southern oceans, feeding upon the abundance of small fish until the time comes to reverse the journey. The total distance traveled in a year by an arctic tern is thus around 22,000 miles (36,000 km). As a result of its journey, it undoubtedly enjoys more hours of sunlight in a year than any other creature on Earth.

The only bird that comes near to the arctic tern in the distances covered in a year is the parasitic jaeger (*Stercorarius parasiticus*), known in Europe as the arctic skua. The American name communicates something of the behavior of this tundra-breeding bird, for it obtains its food by attacking other seabirds, particularly gulls and terns, and harassing them in the air until they regurgitate their stomach contents. The jaeger then leaves off its pursuit to collect the lost food,

*The arctic tern* (Sterna paradisea). *By migrating annually between the Arctic and the Antarctic it spends much of its life in perpetual daylight.* (Photo by Lauri Dammert)

*Emperor penguins (Aptenodytes forsteri) in a colony at Cape Crozier, Antarctica. These are the largest of the penguins, and it is the male that takes sole responsibility for incubating the single egg.* (Photo by Norbert Wu/Minden Pictures)

sometimes even catching it before it lands in the water. These bully birds of the tundra seldom actually attack and kill the birds they pursue but may catch their wings and tails in their bills and cause them much distress. Like the arctic tern, they breed in the open tundra of the Arctic and then migrate southward along the coasts of all the major continents in winter. They may reach as far as New Zealand, southern Australia, and Tierra del Fuego, so they come close to equaling the terns in the distances covered. There is an equivalent Antarctic jaeger, called the south polar skua, which is a general predator of smaller birds, including penguins. It nests on the bleak, boulder-covered coastal regions of Antarctica.

Perhaps the most familiar of the Antarctic birds, however, are the albatrosses (family Diomedeidae) and penguins (family Spheniscidae). Albatrosses are enormous seabirds with wingspans of up to 12 feet (3.5 m). They fly by soaring and gliding, keeping their long wings perfectly stiff and using every updraft from the ocean waves to propel them forward. This is a highly efficient way of flight, involving no flapping, and they can travel great distances in this way. They may cover 5,000 miles (8,000 km) in a week, searching for food for their chicks. Eight different species are frequently found in the southern oceans, but all of them nest on oceanic islands rather than on the mainland of Antarctica.

Penguins, of which there are 17 species, do breed on the coastal strips of the continental mainland of Antarctica. The largest is the emperor penguin (*Aptenodytes forsteri*), with a height of 45 inches (115 cm). Emperor penguins eat fish, swimming underwater with their flipperlike wings and diving for as long as nine minutes at a time. During these dives they can reach depths of 1,300 feet (400 m). Their large size is a great advantage under very cold conditions because they have less surface area (through which body heat is lost) per unit volume than smaller penguins, such as the little penguin (*Eudyptula minor*). The little penguin has a height of just 16 inches (40 cm) and is not nearly as cold-tolerant, breeding no farther south than southern New Zealand. Emperor penguins breed on the bare coastal flats of Antarctica, the male bird being responsible for incubating the single egg, holding it on top of its feet while covering it with a flap of feathered fat. They breed through the Antarctic winter, standing together in large huddles for nine weeks in constant darkness and in temperatures of –76°F (–60°C). They constantly shuffle around the group, which may number as many as 5,000, trying to find the warmest position, and the movement ensures that no individual is exposed on the outside of the congregation for too long.

Penguins, being unable to fly, are permanent residents of the land of ice. They do not have the option of long-distance migration that so many Arctic birds enjoy.

## Polar tundra mammals

The tundra is not rich in mammal diversity, but it does contain some very distinctive species. Like penguins, most mammals are unable to fly, so the opportunities for long-distance migration are limited. Some large mammals undertake regular seasonal movements in the Arctic regions, and bats are exceptional mammals in having the capacity to fly, so they can migrate to a certain extent. But most mammals are forced to cope with the polar winter. Alpine tundra mammals find it easier to move up and down mountains according to the season, so they often adopt this way of life. Relatively few mammals are found in both polar and alpine tundra habitats.

The animal most characteristic of the Arctic tundra is the polar bear (*Ursus maritimus*). This is a massive mammal, often growing to nine feet (2.8 m) in length and 1,500 pounds (700 kg) in weight. It is unusual among bears in being totally carnivorous, feeding mainly upon seals, waiting for them at their breathing holes and snatching them as they surface for air. It is then very happy to consume up to 30 pounds (13 kg) of blubber in one sitting. The polar bear has very thick fur that protects it from the cold and even allows it to spend many hours swimming in the icy polar waters without suffering any harm. The insulating properties of the fur are so efficient that ice forming on the outside fails to melt because the bear's body heat does not penetrate. Even the soles of its feet are covered with hair, preventing frostbite in its toes as it pads across the ice. Its creamy white coloring allows it to blend perfectly into

*The harp seal (Phoca groenlandica) is one of the main prey species of the polar bear. Harp seals breed on ice floes, as shown here in the Gulf of St. Lawrence, where a pup is greeting its mother.* (Photo by Michio Hoshino/ Minden Pictures)

its surroundings of snow and ice floes. Whereas most camouflage in animals is a means of avoiding detection by predators,
in the polar bear it is more likely to be valuable in deceiving its
prey, because it has no predators apart from humans. A white
predator is more likely to be successful in approaching a bask-
ing seal than a dark-colored one. The Inuit people hunt and
eat polar bears, but they do not consume the liver, which is
poisonous because of its exceptionally high level of vitamin A.
The hairs of the polar bear are hollow, which makes them even
better at thermal insulation than solid ones, but the hairs also
allow light energy to penetrate, right through to the black skin
beneath. Here it is absorbed and helps to maintain the bear's
temperature. One problem encountered when polar bears are
kept in southern zoos is the growth of algae within the hollow
hairs, which turns the bear's coat green.

Polar bears spend most of their lives close to the sea, or
even out on the floating ice. There are risks involved in living
on the ice, for it can break up into drifting sections and move
away from land. Polar bears have been recorded on ice floes
as far as 200 miles (320 km) away from land. But their powerful swimming ability enables them to move from one raft to
another and ensures their survival. They seem to be inces-
santly on the move, either in search of prey or, in the case of
males in the spring, in search of a mate. It is at this time of
year that the wandering males are in their most irritable and
dangerous moods and may attack people.

The female polar bear hibernates through the long dark
winter. She burrows beneath the snow, which insulates her
from the worst of the cold conditions, and there she lives off
her fat until the arrival of spring. Females that have become
pregnant as a result of a spring mating give birth to tiny, rat-
size cubs inside the winter den. Although the polar bear is
among the largest of the four-legged carnivores of the world,
its young are among the smallest in relation to the mother's
size. Most commonly, twins are born in December or January.
They suckle on fat-rich milk until they emerge in the spring,
and the female at this stage is in a light state of dormancy
and wakes easily if danger threatens. When they emerge, the
young are weaned onto a diet of meat, usually arctic hare
rather than seal in their first year. The cubs stay with the
mother for the whole of the following summer; she mates

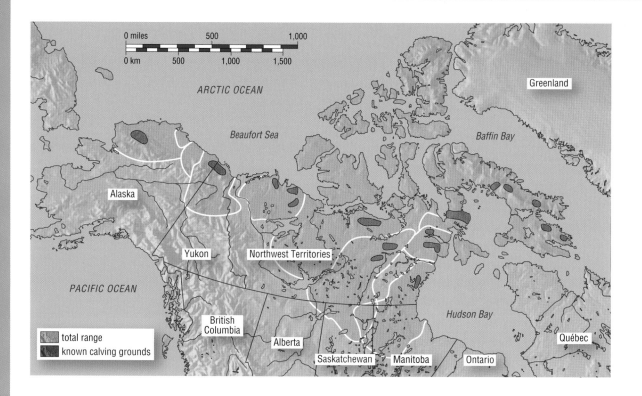

*The range of caribou in the tundra of North America. The species is distributed in a number of herds, each of which occupies its own calving grounds in the spring, migrating south in the winter.*

only every other year. Males, as well as females with growing cubs, tend not to build snow dens, but remain active through the winter.

While polar bears stay in place through the winter and endure the hardships, the caribou (*Rangifer tarandus*) escapes the worst of winter conditions by moving south to areas of better food supply. The caribou, or reindeer as it is called in Europe and Asia, is the only deer that survives north of the Arctic tree line throughout its life. Although there is just one species of caribou, it is widely distributed throughout the polar tundra of the north and is divided into several subspecies that have different ways of life. In Siberia, for example, and also in western North America, there are subspecies that spend their lives in the forest rather than out on the tundra. But the most common forms of this animal graze on the open tundra vegetation. The North American caribou is generally larger than the Eurasian reindeer, a bull often growing to a height of more than four feet (120 cm) at the shoulder and weighing up to 600 pounds (270 kg). The cows are smaller. North America's caribou population occurs in a series of separate herds, each of which has its own preferred calving grounds, as shown in the illustration.

Like the polar bear, caribou are covered in dense hair that is hollow and provides extra thermal insulation. These air-filled hairs also enable the caribou to float very efficiently, and it swims strongly with about a third of its body above the water. In summer the caribou are brown or gray, but they become paler, almost white, in winter, especially on some of the Arctic islands. The hooves have spongy footpads, which effectively spread the weight of the animal and allow it to move over areas of soft, peaty soils without sinking into the mire. In winter, the pads harden and develop bunches of hair, which serve both to insulate the hooves from frost and to give additional grip on the slippery ice and snow. With these adaptations the caribou can run rapidly, achieving speeds of about 50 mph (80 km/h) and can escape such predators as wolves in this way. But the caribou is a sprinter and cannot keep up such a speed for very long, so it may fall prey to wolves if these animals persist in their pursuit until it weakens. Migrating herds

*Caribou* (Rangifer tarandus) *herd with young at its breeding grounds in the tundra of the Alaska National Wildlife Reserve.* (Photo by Michio Hoshino/ Minden Pictures)

of caribou are often accompanied by wolf packs that pick off the old, the fragile, and the young as their victims.

Both male and female caribou have antlers, but those of the male are usually larger. In the North American caribou the antlers can grow to five feet (150 cm) in length. Males fight one another with their antlers during the rutting (breeding) season in the fall, and antlers also provide a means of defense against predators, such as wolves (*Canis lupus*) and wolverines (*Gulo gulo*). After the rut (by about December), the males shed their antlers, but the females retain theirs through the winter, shedding them in April when the calves are born. During the winter, the females are able to assume a degree of dominance because they have retained their antlers, so they can gain better access to the richer vegetation when they are pregnant and need the additional nutrients.

Caribou are very particular about their food. Although they will eat the young leaves of willow and birch, they prefer the new growth of grasses and sedges. They also eat lichens, especially those of the genus *Cladonia,* the so-called reindeer mosses. These small, slow-growing organisms (actually a combination of algae and fungi) are dry and crisp and do not appear very attractive as food, but they are actually quite nutritious. Their very slow growth of about one inch (2.4 cm) every five years means that a grazing herd of caribou can remove many years of growth in a very short time. Consequently the caribou have to keep moving over the tundra to seek out new resources while the grazed areas slowly recover. The outcome is that the tundra can support only low densities of such grazers; a density of one caribou per 150 acres (60 ha) is about as high as can be maintained.

A large proportion of the world's caribou lives in Russia, where almost half of the 3 million or so animals are semidomesticated. Pastoral peoples follow the herds on their migrations, protect them from predators especially in the calving season, and harvest them as a source of milk, meat, and skins. It is likely that caribou were once very much more abundant than they are now, and one estimate indicates that there were once more than 3 million caribou between Hudson Bay and the Mackenzie River. Human predation has undoubtedly contributed to their decline, but they also undergo strong population fluctuations. There has been much research on what

## A tundra heavyweight, the musk ox

The musk ox (*Ovibos moschatus*) is an impressive grazer of the tundra, and this herbivore must rank as one of the most highly adapted of Arctic mammals. It is totally confined to the Arctic tundra, particularly the polar desert regions. Hunting has greatly reduced populations of musk oxen, driving the species to extinction in Alaska by 1860, and the animal has also been eliminated from the Russian Arctic, apart from one island where it has been reintroduced from North America. Musk oxen are now found largely in the Canadian Arctic and Greenland.

Actually more closely related to sheep and goats than to cattle, musk oxen are stocky animals, standing about five feet (1.5 m) in height and weighing up to 670 pounds (300 kg). The musk ox grows a coat of dense shaggy hair, with an undercoating of very soft hair that some Native American tribes use in the construction of cloth. It bears massive horns that curve downward on either side of the head. The musk ox owes its name to its strong smell, which is not in fact due to musk but to its fetid urine. Like caribou, musk oxen are herbivores, but they are more inclined to eat the woody tissues of dwarf shrubs, although they take grasses and sedges during the spring growth. Musk oxen are not migratory but wander around in small groups of about 20 to as many as 100 animals consisting of both males and females. When they are threatened by predators, they form a defensive circle with their heads and formidable horns pointing outward, keeping any young animals safely within the circle. It would take a brave or foolhardy predator to attempt to penetrate the wall of horns that meets it.

causes caribou populations to rise and fall every 60 years or so. Natural and human predation, together with climate and food supply, influence population levels.

Of all the animals of the Arctic tundra, few have generated more interest or legend than the lemming (family Microtidae). These small rodents have a reputation for mass suicide; folk tradition asserts that lemmings leap from cliffs by the hundreds during episodes of population explosion. There are several different species of lemmings, all of them small rodents that survive under very extreme conditions of cold. The one that has generated most of the fabulous stories of suicide is the Norwegian lemming (*Lemmus lemmus*), which occupies the mountainous tundra of Scandinavia. It is certainly true that the populations of the Norwegian lemming undergo very considerable fluctuations, and there are years in which large numbers of the animals migrate in massive numbers, usually down the valleys from their mountain homes. When they reach a water barrier, Norwegian lemmings are often undecided what to do because, although they swim quite well, they are reluctant to take to water unless they can clearly see the other side. The pressure of the crowd at such times undoubtedly forces many individuals off the edge of cliffs or riverbanks and into the water, where they drown. The discovery of large numbers of drowned lemmings washed up on the shores of fjords is probably what inspired the stories of mass suicide.

Exactly what causes the population explosions among lemmings is still not entirely clear. There is an approximate three- to four-year cycle in the population fluctuations. When the population is at its peak size, there may be as many as 160 lemmings in each acre of tundra (400/ha). The buildup in population probably results from an abundance of high-quality food. During low lemming years the grazing pressure is much diminished and the vegetation grows more rapidly. The growing vegetation then becomes richer in certain essential elements that are in short supply, such as phosphorus. The outcome is a lemming plague that consumes the resources, so the population crashes once again as quality food becomes scarce. During the stage when food resources are beginning to run low, the lemmings migrate outward from their centers of population, giving rise to the myths associated with them. In peak population years, the lemming is a major source of food to a wide range of predators, including snowy owl, arctic fox, rough-legged hawk (*Buteo lagopus*), and pomarine (*Stercorarius pomarinus*) and long-tailed jaegers (*Stercorarius longicaudus*). These predators also undergo population cycles that match the lemming cycles, illustrating how dependent they are upon this source of food. Snowy owls, for example, raise as many as 10 or more young in a good lemming year but may fail to rear any when lemming populations are low. It is unlikely that the intensity of predation actually causes the crash in lemming populations, however. Even heavy predation is likely to account for only about 10 percent of the lemming population, which is hardly enough to cause a population crash; food limitation is much more likely to be the cause. A drop in the availability of food would affect the rate of reproduction, which would have a rapid impact on the overall population of the lemmings.

Like most other small mammals, lemmings are capable of very rapid breeding. Unlike many of the other small rodents of the tundra (such as voles), they have the remarkable ability to breed all year. In one study of brown lemmings (*Lemmus sibiricus*), 33 percent of females were found to be pregnant in the December-to-April period and about 80 percent in July. The arctic lemming (*Dicrostonyx torquatus*) has even higher rates of breeding, with 40 percent of females pregnant in winter and 90 percent in July.

In the Arctic summer, of course, there is no opportunity for nocturnal activity to avoid the bird predators that mainly hunt by daylight. As the summer wears on, however, the lemmings tend to confine their activity to the hours of darkness to avoid the attention of birds and foxes. Lemmings are herbivores, and the different species have varying food preferences, which is why they are able to coexist in the same area. The arctic lemming, for example, prefers broad-leaved herbs and dwarf willows, and it eats very little in the way of grasses, sedges, mosses, and lichens. The brown lemming, on the other hand, concentrates on these latter plants and takes very little of the broad-leaved and woody plants. In winter lemmings burrow beneath the snow and the breeding females construct well-insulated nests of sedge stalks to protect themselves against the penetrating cold.

Another grazing mammal of the tundra is the arctic hare (*Lepus arcticus*), which has the most northerly distribution of any of the world's hares and rabbits (lagomorphs). It occurs in the tundra regions between Labrador and the Mackenzie River, being replaced in Alaska by the Alaska hare (*Lepus othus*). The arctic hare is one of the largest of the hares, weighing around 12 pounds (5.5 kg). It is quite fussy about its food, concentrating upon arctic willow (*Salix arctica*), which means that its distribution is limited by this particular food species. It is quite unusual in such a harsh environment to have a large herbivore that is so strictly limited in its food preferences, but it seems to thrive despite this specialized diet. The arctic hare remains active through the winter and therefore has to cope with extreme cold in the months of darkness, often with monthly average temperatures of –35°F (–38°C). Unlike the lemming, which burrows below the snow, it has to survive without any insulation apart from its thick fur. Its breeding, however, is restricted to the summer, and it produces a litter of five or six young in a scraped hollow, often in the shelter of a rock. The female arctic hare is a more devoted mother than is the case with most lagomorphs. She remains with the young for as long as two or three weeks; then they form small groups or crèches and the mothers return regularly to nurse their own offspring. After about nine weeks the young are left to fend for themselves. Adult arctic hares remain quite solitary during the summer, but in the fall they form large herds. Flocks numbering into the hundreds have been recorded on Ellesmere Island, and this may offer them some protection against such predators as the arctic foxes, which find it difficult to stalk a grazing flock without being detected. The hare herds can cause intensive grazing pressure on the tundra vegetation and may outcompete some of their fellow grazers, such as musk oxen and caribou, especially in years of high populations. Like lemmings, they exhibit a cyclic pattern of population variation, but with peak populations roughly every nine years.

In Europe and Asia the mountain hare, or blue hare (*Lepus timidus*), is found. This is closely related to the arctic hare but is unusual among tundra mammals in being found also in the more southerly mountains of Europe, including the Alps. It is called the "blue hare" because its summer coat is a blue-gray color, but in winter it molts and produces a white coat with just the tips of the ears remaining black. It has a wider range of food preferences than the arctic hare, feeding on grasses and heathers. The change in coat color is of obvious advantage in habitats that are dark in summer and white in winter, but the timing of the molt is crucial in determining how effectively this camouflage defends the animal against predators. A combination of day length and temperature determines the onset of the molt, but if the timing is wrong because of early snow in fall, for example, then the outcome can be fatal. White hares on the dark surface of the snowless tundra, or gray hares on the surface of the snow, are easily spotted by the foxes and eagles that prey upon them.

One group of mammals that may not immediately spring to mind in the context of the tundra is bats (family Vespertilionidae). It is certainly true that bats are scarcer and less diverse in the tundra regions than they are in the temperate and tropical regions, but they do occur as seasonal migrants, taking advantage of the great abundance of insects found in the Arctic summer. Bats are nocturnal insectivores, flying and hunting at night to avoid the effects of daytime predation by such birds as hawks and falcons. By confining their activity to dusk and nighttime, they also avoid direct competition with insect-eating birds, such as swallows and swifts. In the Arctic, of course, bats are faced with the problem of the absence of any real night during the summer. Studies on bat activity times in northern Norway have shown that they maintain a period of hunting that corresponds with their perceived "night," generally between 10 P.M. and 2 A.M. During that period the activity of bird insectivores is also much lower, so the bats and the birds still seem to divide the available time between them despite the absence of darkness as a cue. This division is not ideal for bats, however. Insect activity is lower at "night" even though the Sun is still above the horizon. So the bats have the poorest slot for their insect hunting and yet are still exposed to attack by bird predators. It is not surprising that bats are scarce in the tundra.

The mammals of the Antarctic are entirely marine rather than true tundra species. Whales, dolphins, porpoises, seals, and sea lions spend most or all of their lives in the oceans or, in the case of the seals, on nearby beaches and ice floes. No land mammals have been able to colonize or survive on this extremely inhospitable continent.

## Alpine tundra mammals

Relatively few mammal species are found in both polar and alpine tundra, except where mountain chains connect the two, as in the North American Rocky Mountains and the mountain ridge of central Norway. The wolverine has a range that extends from the Arctic tundra south into the United States along the Rocky Mountain chain, and the Norwegian

*Pair of yellow-bellied marmots* (Marmota flaviventris) *in Yellowstone National Park, Wyoming. These alpine tundra mammals are herbivores and build up enough fat during the short summer to enable them to hibernate through the long winter.* (Photo by Carolyn McKendry/ IstockPhoto)

lemming is found on mountains over the whole length of Norway. The mountain hare is unusual in being found both in the tundra of the Arctic and also on isolated, more southerly mountains, such as the Alps. On the whole, the mountains of the world support their own distinctive mammal communities.

One of the most typical of mountain mammals is the marmot (*Marmota* species). There are, in fact, many species of marmot and they are widely distributed around the mountains of the world, including the Rockies, the Alps, and right across to Siberia. They are not large mammals, generally about two feet (60 cm) in length, although the hoary marmot (*Marmota caligata*) of western Canada can grow to almost three feet (90 cm). What they lack in length, they make up in girth, being rotund animals with a stocky build. Marmots are closely related to the squirrels and, like them, are herbivorous, spending the summer grazing on the herbage of the alpine tundra above the tree line. They enjoy well-drained, sloping grassland, often with rocky outcrops and scree, where they will sit and watch the skies for predatory eagles and give warning to their grazing colleagues by emitting loud and penetrating whistles when they see danger threatening.

Marmots are largely social and cooperative mammals, living in extended family groups, but they defend their local territory and will chase off individuals that seek to graze their territory. Males will also wrestle with one another during the breeding season, standing on their back legs and pushing one another with their forelegs. They live in burrows or rock crevices beneath the ground, and they have short, strong limbs for burrowing in the rocky soils. Here they hibernate through the long cold winter. Once the spring arrives and the melting snow reveals green plants, the marmots emerge, bask in the sunlight, and clean themselves. They are active in the daytime and are relatively unafraid of people, so they are easy to observe in their activities. One of their first activities on emerging in the spring is to clear out their bedding and replace it with clean materials. When a marmot tries to carry too much new bedding material, it may end up rolling on its back holding a mass of bedding with all four legs. When this happens, its companions drag it by the tail into their burrow. This behavior was first recorded by the Roman naturalist Pliny (23–79 C.E.) from his observations in the European Alps, and, like some of Pliny's other tales, it was once regarded as suspect. But scientists in recent times have observed the same behavior, so Pliny's unlikely-sounding story has been confirmed. When their winter bedding has been replaced, marmots turn their minds to breeding, and the first young are born within about six weeks of mating. The family stays together for several years before the young are sufficiently mature to set off on their own.

In the short season of the high mountain tundra, the marmot must spend much of its time feeding, especially as the winter approaches. Marmots do not store food in their burrows but build up large reserves of fat to keep them alive through the hibernation. This, together with their dense fur, serves as an insulating layer to retain some body warmth, and human hunters prize both the fur and the fat. The black-capped marmot (*Marmota camschatica*) of eastern Russia is one of the most proficient sleepers in the animal kingdom. It can spend up to nine months of every year asleep.

By mid-September it is covered with a thick layer of fat and weighs about 11 pounds (5 kg). It descends into its burrow, along with the other members of its family, and they curl into a tight ball with their forepaws covering the sides of their heads. As the external temperature drops, so does the body temperature of the marmot, often becoming as low as 40°F (4°C) and sometimes even below freezing. At this stage, it is very difficult to detect any sign of life in the animal. Its heart beats just once every two or three minutes, and it breathes only once every 10 minutes. Even this very low level of body activity does generate some waste materials, so the marmot warms up and wakes about every three weeks so that it can urinate. By the time it finally wakes in May, it has lost half of its body weight, so it is easy to appreciate its eagerness to emerge and start eating. The marmots are a group of mammals that are essentially alpine tundra rather than polar tundra in distribution. The same can be said of the sheep and goats; many of these are mammals of the mountains.

The American mountain goat (*Oreamnos americanus*) is actually not a true goat but belongs somewhere between the goats and the antelopes. It occurs above the tree line in the mountains of Alaska, British Columbia, and the Rocky Mountains south into Colorado, and South Dakota. Like those of many of its relatives, its hoof is adapted for gripping, having a hard outer rim and a softer inner part that can grip slippery surfaces. It lives on the high, steep, and inaccessible cliffs of the mountains, producing young in the spring that are able to climb on the precipices virtually from birth. The kids may fall prey to golden eagles, but their greatest danger is death by misadventure. A slip on a mountain ledge, or a loose rock, can easily lead to a fatal fall. The chamois (*Rupicapra rupicapra*) of the European and western Asian mountains is a close relative of the American mountain goat and has many of the same adaptations. Like the wild goat, it is polygamous and the males compete for harems of females in the November rutting season. The chamois has been extensively hunted in Europe but is now widely protected and is becoming a frequently seen animal of the Alps and Pyrenees. It can live up to 22 years and is capable of survival at very high altitudes, the highest on record being 15,430 feet (4,750 m) on Mont Blanc, Europe's highest mountain.

Another agile rock-climbing mammal of the American mountains is the bighorn sheep (*Ovis canadensis*). It occupies the more remote areas of the Rockies and the Sierras, avoiding contact with human beings. It lives in groups, consisting of up to 15 animals (mostly females and young) in summer and congregating into herds of up to 100 for the winter. The males join the female groups during the rut, when battles for access to females reach epic proportions. Competing males charge one another head-on, and the crash of their colliding horns can be heard a mile away. The heads of the males have a very dense cover of bone at the front, so a direct clash rarely causes any serious injury. These battles may last many hours until the fitter male wins the day and has the privilege of passing on his genes to the next generation. The lambs are susceptible to predation, particularly from golden eagles and mountain lions. Wolves, coyotes, bears, bobcats, and lynx can also pose a threat to them if they wander from their precipitous habitats into lower parts of valleys. Bighorn sheep tend to migrate from the higher regions that they occupy in the summer, feeding on grasses and sedges, to the lower parts of the mountain in winter, where woody materials including willow form their major food. Like the chamois, the bighorn has been intensively hunted in the past, but such activities are now carefully controlled to ensure its long-term survival.

There are species of mountain sheep in Asia, but on the whole these tend to be animals of rolling hills rather than steep cliffs and rocky crags. The nearest equivalent to the bighorn is the snow sheep (*Ovis nivicola*) of the eastern Asian mountains, which extend into the northern highlands beyond the Arctic Circle. In most of the Eurasian mountains, however, the ecological equivalent to the bighorn sheep is a type of goat, the ibex (*Capra ibex*). It is a large goat, up to three feet (90 cm) in height and notable for its conspicuous, backward-curving horns, often around 30 inches (75 cm) in length. The horns are black and strongly ridged, and, as with bighorn sheep, they are used in battles between males during the rutting season. Human hunters almost drove the alpine ibex to extinction, partly for the trophies supplied by their enormous horns, but also for the so-called bezoar stone. The animal's stomach contains this hard concretion of undigested material. People believed that this "stone" possessed great potential for healing, including the cure for various types of poisoning, and slaughtered the animals to obtain it. Fortunately, when the population had been reduced to just a small herd in northern Italy, authorities imposed protection and instigated a program of reintroduction over its former range. The scattered populations of ibex are now growing once again.

In general, the mammals of the world's mountains have suffered more from human hunting than those of the polar tundra. Mountains are more accessible to people and consequently their mammalian inhabitants more vulnerable. As tourism and mineral harvesting develop in the polar regions, disturbance, habitat loss, and hunting may well intensify there too.

## Adaptations in tundra mammals

The mammals of both polar and alpine tundra face similar stresses. Periods of very low temperature are common to both habitats, and the survival of any animal depends upon its being adequately equipped to deal with this problem. As a consequence, many animals of the tundra share a number of general features:

1. Although size varies (from lemmings to musk oxen) all of the animals tend to be compact and rounded, having relatively small extremities, such as tails and ears. Tundra animals need to maintain a blood supply to their extremities to keep them warm and avoid frostbite, and a rounded form is most efficient in maintaining body temperature and avoiding heat loss. Even birds, such as penguins, are large and somewhat rounded.

2. An abundance of hair ensures that the hot skin of mammals, richly supplied with blood vessels, resists heat loss to the surrounding cold air. This works by trapping a layer of air close to the skin that becomes warm but is not easily removed. Many tundra animals have hollow hairs, which are even more efficient than solid hairs in holding in the warmth. Hairiness is also a feature of many tundra insects, including butterflies and bumblebees. In birds, of course, it is replaced by feathers.

3. Changing color with the season, usually white in winter and a darker color in summer, has many advantages in terms of camouflage. It also lets an animal absorb heat from the Sun more effectively in summer and avoids the problem of radiating energy in winter. Blue hares and arctic foxes are examples of tundra animals that change color seasonally.

4. Hibernation is a means of reducing the biochemical activity of the body in times of severe cold, and this permits an animal to reduce to zero its requirement for food and allows it to survive on its accumulated fat reserves. It leads to problems of waste disposal, but the greatly reduced levels of body activity solve these.

5. Migration is an alternative to hibernation that allows an animal to take advantage of the resources of the tundra in its productive summer and avoid the stresses of its unproductive winter. In the case of mountain tundra animals, this may involve movements up and down the mountain with the changing seasons.

6. Summer breeding is the general rule with Arctic mammals, but some of the most successful species, like the lemming, have mastered the art of year-round breeding. This is possible only for a small animal that is able to create its own microclimate beneath a protective layer of snow. Winter production of young (as in polar bears and emperor penguins) has the advantage that the young are sufficiently grown by the time they emerge from winter dens to be able to take full advantage of the short summer season for their feeding and further growth.

7. Many tundra species have relatively wide distributions compared with the plants and animals in other parts of the world. The mountain avens (*Dryas octopetala*), the white-fronted goose, and the polar bear are examples of plant and animal species that are found throughout the Arctic regions of Russia, Alaska, Canada, Greenland, and Scandinavia. It is important to remember, however, that the distances between continents are not as great as might be assumed from conventional maps. Representations of the surface of the Earth (a sphere) on a flat piece of paper tend to exaggerate the size of the polar

regions. The total length of latitude 70° is actually only one-third that of the equator.

The animals and plants of the tundra regions of the world have thus come to share a number of structural, physiological, and biogeographical adaptations to their common problem, life in a frigid climate.

## Conclusions

Intensely cold conditions cause all chemical reactions to proceed slowly, and this includes those occurring within living cells. For organisms that cannot control their body temperature (which includes all microbes, plants, and invertebrate animals) activity in the tundra is confined to those occasions when the temperature rises in summer. Wind, burial by snow, and even drought can add to the stresses of life in the tundra.

Tundra plants are generally herbs or dwarf shrubs, frequently take on a cushion form, and are often evergreen. Trees are absent, and annual plants are extremely rare. There is a short season for flowering, and pollinating insects may not be abundant, so there is much competition to attract their attention. Consequently, flowers are often large and brightly colored, especially among species of alpine tundra. Many plants have hairy surfaces and cells rich in chemical antifreezes, which enable them to survive the winter cold.

Tundra soils are often rich in undecomposed organic matter, so there is plenty of food available for microbes, but for much of the year the temperature is too low for these organisms to be active. Even in summer, many parts of the tundra become too wet for decomposer microbes to operate efficiently. Lichens are among the most successful groups of microbes. The combination of photosynthetic (cyanobacteria or algae) and structural (fungi) components allows them to grow slowly, fix nitrogen, and avoid desiccation in summer.

Invertebrate animals abound during the summertime. They include soil dwellers that feed on the organic debris, herbivores that consume the growing vegetation, pollen feeders, and predators. Tundra wetland provides a rich habitat for many aquatic insects, such as mosquitoes.

Birds take advantage of the brief tundra summer for breeding, many of them migrating from distant regions. In the polar tundra the long days allow birds extended time in which to feed their young. Seabirds, wetland birds, and wading birds are abundant, but there are also resident bird species, including herbivorous ptarmigans and predatory falcons and owls.

Few mammals are found in both polar and tundra habitats. Mammals of the Antarctic tundra include many that are mainly marine but come ashore to breed, including seals. The Arctic has a much larger range of mammals including herbivores, such as lemmings and caribou, and predators, such as arctic fox and polar bear. The alpine tundra is the home of several species of marmot and also of various sheep and goat species. These are adapted to life in steep and inaccessible places, where they can avoid predation by humans.

The diversity of animals, plants, and microbes found in the tundra is undoubtedly lower than in other major biomes, but that does not reduce the scientific interest or the value of this biome. The living organisms of the tundra face some of the most severe conditions to be found on Earth. Only a volcanic crater could be regarded as more inhospitable than these frigid regions, yet life in abundance is found there. The species that survive demand admiration, for they have achieved something that very few humans have been prepared to face, namely living in the tundra. These species represent highly tuned products of evolution that show an extraordinary set of adaptations to their harsh environment. In their structure, their biochemistry, and their behavior, they have managed to develop strategies for survival, and humans can learn much from them that would be of great value. Low biodiversity in the tundra, therefore, does not mean low value.

# CHAPTER 5

# HISTORY OF THE TUNDRA

Tundra can exist only in extremely cold conditions, so the question "How old is the tundra?" is really asking how long the Earth has known such cold episodes. The answer is that coldness has a very long history on this planet; on the other hand, it has been a relatively rare experience. Cold periods have occurred perhaps nine or 10 times in the history of the Earth, but these times of cold are the exception rather than the rule.

## Ice ages

The occasions in the Earth's history when permanent ice has been present in the form of ice sheets and glaciers are often referred to as *ice ages*. They rarely last more than a few million years, which is quite brief in relation to the 4.6 billion–year history of the Earth, and these ice ages are not times of uniform cold but are often interrupted by relatively warm episodes. So an ice age consists of alternating cold and warm conditions. A time of cold, when ice sheets and glaciers spread, is called a *glacial,* and a warmer episode when ice retreats is called an *interglacial.*

The accompanying table shows the occasions when ice ages have occurred on Earth. An approximate reconstruction of the climatic history of the Earth is given in the graph at right.

Past ice ages have left evidence behind them in the rocks. As discussed in chapter 2, the movement of ice over the surface of the ground and its subsequent melting leave behind distinct clues (see "Effects of glaciation," pages 40–43). Some of these clues are the scars that they create on the landscape, but that kind of evidence does not survive the millions of years involved here. Glaciers also leave distinct deposits, such

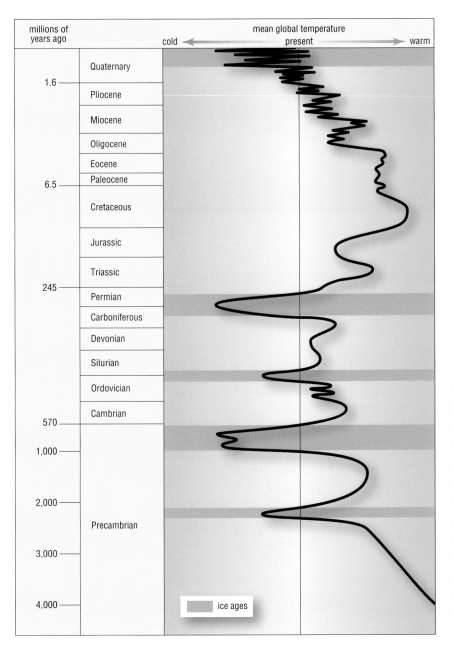

| millions of years ago | | mean global temperature |
|---|---|---|

cold ← present → warm

| | Quaternary |
|---|---|
| 1.6 | Pliocene |
| | Miocene |
| | Oligocene |
| | Eocene |
| 6.5 | Paleocene |
| | Cretaceous |
| | Jurassic |
| | Triassic |
| 245 | Permian |
| | Carboniferous |
| | Devonian |
| | Silurian |
| | Ordovician |
| 570 | Cambrian |
| 1,000 | Precambrian |
| 2,000 | |
| 3,000 | |
| 4,000 | |

ice ages

*The changes in global temperature (black line) over geological time, determined from chemical and biological evidence. The wide blue bands represent the ice ages, the times in Earth's history when glaciers and ice sheets and hence the tundra biome were present. Note that the time axis has been expanded for more recent times.*

as boulder clays, or tills, which can become effectively "fossilized." These tills may be buried by subsequent sediments and incorporated into rocks, and they are then called *tillites* to distinguish them from more recent glacial deposits. These tillites have been found in Precambrian rocks dating from

# The occurrence of ice ages in the history of the Earth

| Era | Geological period | Approximate time of occurrence |
|-----|-------------------|-------------------------------|
| Cenozoic | Pliocene/Pleistocene | 10 million–10,000 years ago |
| Mesozoic | Jurassic | 150 million years ago |
| Paleozoic | Carboniferous/Permian | 300 million years ago |
| | Ordovician | 450 million years ago |
| Proterozoic (Precambrian) | | 600 million years ago |
| | | 750 million years ago |
| | | 900 million years ago |
| | | 2,300 million years ago |

Note: Here the term *ice ages* is used to indicate times when ice sheets (and therefore tundra habitats) have been present on Earth.

billions of years ago, showing that ice ages have occurred right from the very early history of the Earth. The Earth is considered to be about 4.6 billion years old. From around 3.8 billion years ago, the first true rocks were being formed and the very first living organisms were present on the planet. Between then and 2.3 billion years ago there was at least one ice age, and possibly as many as three. It is very difficult to construct a precise climatic history of the Earth at such an ancient stage in its development, but it is certain that the Earth was already occasionally experiencing a sufficiently cold climate to result in the formation of glaciers in at least some parts of the world. These early ice ages are not shown in the graph because their precise timing and duration are so uncertain.

The timing of ice ages, particularly the more recent ones, which are better recorded in the geological strata and better dated, shows a distinct periodicity. The overall pattern suggests a cycle in which cold periods alternate with warmer ones. The Earth seems to experience ice ages roughly every 150 million years, but as yet, no one has come up with a fully acceptable explanation of the mechanism that causes this long-term regularity. Many theories have been put forward to explain why the Earth might occasionally develop glaciers and ice caps, and these ideas are extremely varied. The Earth's crust consists of a series of plates that are constantly on the move, sometimes separating the landmasses and sometimes leading to collisions. It is possible that the configuration and spacing of the plates is involved in determining ice ages. Perhaps there have to be large landmasses in the right position (which is not necessarily at the poles) for ice to begin forming. The appropriate location would have to be cold (therefore close to the poles) but also where the precipitation is high, permitting the abundant snowfall to form ice (which means some distance away from the poles, which are virtually deserts). Ocean currents also play an important part. These help to distribute heat energy (ultimately derived from the Sun) over the surface of the planet, and any disruption to the circulation of these currents could lead to an ice age. Again, the right positioning of continents could do precisely this by modifying the direction in which warm waters flow. When mountain ranges arise, they lead to changes in precipitation patterns and create high landforms where glaciers can form. Finally, there is always the possibility that astronomical factors are involved, such as the distance between the Earth and the Sun, or the angle of the Earth upon its axis. Further geological research may help to sort out exactly what causes the Earth to enter an ice age at certain points in its history.

## Glacial history

Although the present conditions on Earth are relatively warm, there is no reason to believe that the ice age of Pliocene and Pleistocene times is over. It is entirely likely that the present warmth is simply the latest interglacial in a continuing ice age. More is known about this current ice age than any other, simply because the records have been better preserved than for any previous cold episode. This ice age has so far lasted about 10 million years, beginning in the Miocene, becoming more evident in the Pliocene, and then really making its mark on the Earth during the last 1.8 million years of the Pleistocene.

It may come as a surprise that an ice age continues despite all the current discussions of global warming. Ice sheets and tundra are still present, however, and the possibility remains that they may one day expand again. During the past 10,000 years (a mere blink of the eye in geological terms), conditions have been warm and ice caps and glaciers have retreated far from their former positions. There have been many warm interruptions to the general cold of the last couple of million years, however, and there is no reason to believe that the present warm period is anything more that another such interruption. The cyclic pattern of recent history, in which cold and warm episodes have alternated, suggests that the cold will return. To be able to predict the behavior of the world climate is obviously very important to people, so understanding the detailed pattern of climate change—and with it the fate of the tundra biome—is an important area of scientific research.

Geologists divide the history of the Earth into convenient sections, trying to use "natural" breaks wherever possible. These are points where the fossil content of the rocks changes relatively abruptly, often indicating a sudden change in the climate or other conditions on Earth. The separation of the Cretaceous period from the Tertiary period some 65 million years ago is a good example of a natural break because the dinosaur fossils disappear and other groups of organisms exhibit considerable change at that point. This boundary is now believed to have been caused by a catastrophic cosmic event, specifically the collision of a massive meteor, or bolide, from space onto the surface of the Earth. The kind of abrupt and cataclysmic environmental change that resulted from this catastrophe, however, is relatively rare, and the divisions of geological time are usually far less abrupt and less easy to identify. This is certainly the case with the progression of the current ice age, involving the formation of permanent ice caps and the development of glaciers in various parts of the world. Although ice began to appear back in the Miocene, the first evidence for extensive glaciation occurs in the late Pliocene, especially after about 2.4 million years ago, and cold conditions became even more acute around 1.8 million years ago, which is generally regarded as the beginning of the Quaternary period and the Pleistocene epoch within that period. But there is still much argument about this, and some geologists feel that the change at 2.4 million years would be a better marker for the beginning of the Pleistocene. This argument illustrates that Earth's cooling over the last few million years has been gradual and that any subdivision is somewhat artificial and arbitrary.

Naturally, much more is known about the Pleistocene glaciations than about the older glacial events. Yet it is not so long ago that the idea of any past glaciation was unheard of in scientific debate. In the 18th century, when great advances were being made in many of the physical sciences, geology was still in its infancy. A Scottish scientist, James Hutton (1726–97), should perhaps be regarded as the father of geology as a science, and he developed a very important concept called uniformitarianism. This simply means that past events can be interpreted by studying what is going on in the present, because the mechanisms involved are essentially the same. This may seem obvious to a modern reader, but it was quite a novel way of thinking in the late 18th century. The history of the Earth was considered to be the outcome of a series of abrupt and unrepeatable events, such as the biblical Creation and the Flood of Noah. The features of geology, including fossils, landforms, sedimentary rocks, and so on, were interpreted entirely within the framework of these catastrophic events. Hutton proposed that the erosion of mountains and valleys could be accounted for by the gradual action of streams and rivers and that the timescales involved, although extremely long, could be calculated by simple mathematics.

The idea was taken up by the British geologist Charles Lyell (1797–1875), whose work greatly influenced his close friend Charles Darwin (1809–82). Like many geologists at the time, he was concerned with the problem of how some rocks (erratics) were found far from their source areas, despite being massive in size and very difficult to move. What mechanism available on Earth today could account for such movements? The great Flood of Noah had been used to account for these in the past, but could water movements have shifted such large objects? Lyell wondered whether they might have been transported in icebergs floating on the floodwaters.

It is not surprising that the real advances in the understanding of ice and ice movements came from the mountainous country of Switzerland. The Swiss geologist Louis Agassiz

(1807–73) grew up in a land of glaciers, U-shaped valleys, hanging valleys, moraines, and ice-scratched rocks (see "Effects of glaciation," pages 40–43). In 1837, he presented a research paper to the Swiss Society of Natural Sciences in which he came to the logical, but extremely novel, conclusion that the glaciers he knew so well had been much more extensive in times past than they were in his day. He coined the term *Eiszeit,* the German equivalent of "ice age," and proposed that there had been such a cold event in the geologically recent past.

Others at that time were making similarly radical claims, but they were often regarded as somewhat unbalanced. Some German geologists, for example, claimed in the 1830s that Arctic ice had once extended as far south as Germany, but their views were ridiculed. Then Agassiz stepped in and confidently stated that ice masses from the far north had not only entered Germany but also had covered much of northwestern Europe, parts of Asia, and the northern regions of North America. American geologists accepted the ideas of Agassiz much more readily than those of the other Europeans, and in 1846 Harvard University invited him to take up the Chair of Geology. From there he conducted pioneering work on the glaciation of North America, although arguments about his very controversial ideas continued well into the 1860s.

The next question to be answered, once the concept of a past ice age was well established, was whether it had been one single event or whether there had actually been several ice ages. Agassiz tended to assume that a global ice expansion had taken place on just one occasion, but work being conducted in southeast England showed that there were several different types of boulder clays, or tills, that could be distinguished from one another by the alignment of the stones embedded within them. These different tills must have been laid down during separate glacial advances, each moving in a different direction. Workers in Scotland also found fossil evidence that there had been warm intervals between the glacial advances.

Geological studies in the European Alps also made it evident that the recent ice age consisted of more than one glacial advance and retreat. In 1909 this work dealing with the Alps was formally published, proposing that there had been four main ice advances. The publication named these after the rivers Gunz, Mindel, Riss, and Würm, all of which are tributaries of central Europe's Danube River, and it identified the rivers as the advance limits of the different glacial stages. For about 50 years, this interpretation of the climatic fluctuations of the Pleistocene was regarded as firmly established, and geologists attempted to fit all new evidence into this framework. But in science, the test of time often proves new ideas to be wrong or too simple, and such was the case with this fourfold interpretation of the Pleistocene. With the development of more sophisticated techniques for the study of climate change, such as the use of oxygen isotopes in marine sediments and in ice cores, it became evident that the true picture is much more complicated. Within the past million years there have indeed been at least a dozen major glacials, interspersed with warm interglacials. But shorter-term fluctuations have taken place within these stages as the climate has displayed a high degree of instability. These shorter intervals of cold and warmth, which are too short or too insignificant to permit major biological responses, are termed *stadials* and *interstadials,* respectively, rather than *glacials* and *interglacials*—terms that are reserved for major changes in climate resulting in major biological responses, such as the extension of polar tundra during the cold intervals and the expansion of forests in the warm ones, including the present interglacial.

This understanding of the complexity of climatic fluctuations in the Pleistocene has emerged only since about 1970, and much still remains to be discovered about its precise pattern, the dating of the glacial advances, the causes of the observed fluctuations, and the biological and ecological consequences of these changes. Research is currently focused on the periodicity of warm and cold episodes in the hope of clarifying the pattern of change (see sidebar on page 138) and providing a basis for future forecasting.

Detailed study of the older glacial episodes is difficult because so much of the evidence has been destroyed by the more recent ones. Every time the glaciers advance they are

## Cycles of climate change

Using a range of physical and chemical techniques, including the rate at which certain radioactive compounds in the rocks decay, scientists have now worked out the general timescale of events in the Pleistocene. The "wavelength" of the glacial/interglacial cycles (involving one full cycle of cold and warm stages) of the past million years has been about 100,000 years, with the warm episodes occupying only a relatively small proportion of this time span. The change from warm to cold is usually quite gradual, involving a series of steadily intensifying cold episodes, so glacial advances probably take place in a series of stages interrupted by minor retreats. The glacial maximum is eventually achieved late in the cold part of the cycle, followed by relatively rapid warming, with the maximum warmth of the interglacial being achieved within around 5,000 to 10,000 years, after which cooling begins again.

This general pattern seems to have applied to the majority of the glacial episodes of the later Pleistocene, and it is interesting to note that Earth is 10,000 years into the present interglacial, so according to the established pattern, things should be on the cooling run by now. Perhaps the planet was moving in this direction before the global warming of the past 150 years began when human industrial activities started to pump carbon dioxide into the atmosphere. We may be holding the next glaciation at bay.

likely to carve away many of the tills and other evidence laid down in former times. In the case of the most recent glaciation, the evidence remains more fully intact. Glacial advances have taken different directions, however, so that some previously glaciated regions have been left undamaged. This means that the evidence of earlier glaciations remains undisturbed and can be used to reconstruct the patterns of past glaciation. The study of recent glacial movements (those of the last 40,000 years) has been greatly assisted by the development of the radiocarbon method of dating. This method depends upon the gradual decay of heavy, unstable atoms of carbon into their normal, lighter form. The decay occurs at a constant rate, so the content of heavy carbon in any organic material gives a reasonable estimate of its age. Using this and other dating methods, it has been possible to reconstruct the history of the ice, and hence the tundra, in some detail for these recent times.

The last major glaciation (called the Wisconsin Glacial in North America) reached its greatest extent only 22,000 years ago, which is very recent in geological terms. By 14,000 years ago it was beginning to melt in response to a rapid rise in the temperature of the planet. The evidence for this warming is obtained mainly from the sediments laid down in lakes that formed around the margins of the melting ice. The mud that settled in these lakes contained portions of dead plants and animals that were preserved there, and these provide a detailed record of the vegetation and animal life of the region at the time. Where once there was ice, tundra appeared. Abundant pollen from grasses, sedges and other Arctic herbs and shrubs was preserved in the mud. Scientists can extract the pollen grains from sediment cores, identify them, and count them to supply a picture of the vegetation that followed the melting ice northward. In places dwarf shrubs and even fully developed trees, especially birch, became abundant. But around the Atlantic seaboard, especially in the eastern Atlantic, on the European mainland, there is strong evidence for a sudden drop in temperature back to glacial conditions between 10,800 and 10,000 years ago on the radiocarbon timescale. Not only does the tree and shrub pollen vanish from the record, the very nature of the lake sediment changes. Instead of the organic mud formed by the productive growth of aquatic plants, gray clay and stone fragments appear, indicating severe climate and the erosion of bare soils into lake basins. Clearly, conditions became so cold during this short episode that there was a return to permafrost and unstable soils that slid down slopes over the frozen subsoil each summer.

There was also a return to the growth of glaciers, but this cold period was short and should be regarded as a stadial rather than a true glacial episode. Very rapid warming followed; the evidence from fossils of highly mobile animals, such as flying beetles, which are able to take rapid advantage of a change in climate, suggests that the temperature rose by around 9°F or 10°F (5°C) within a matter of a decade or so. This is a very sudden change in climate, and it illustrates just how quickly conditions on Earth can alter. But why did conditions change? Exactly what was taking place that could cause such massive changes in climate? These are important questions because the answers will help us understand the mechanisms that underlie climate function.

One widely accepted theory about the cause of the stadial at the close of the Wisconsin glaciation is that the melting of the ice over North America actually caused the return of cold conditions. At the height of the Wisconsin Glacial, an enormous ice sheet (the Laurentide Ice Sheet) covered much of what is now Canada and the northern part of the United States. As this began to melt, the large volume of water produced flowed mainly southward into the Gulf of Mexico. As the ice retreated, however, an alternative outlet became available, namely the St. Lawrence River leading into the North Atlantic. The sudden flushing of large quantities of cold freshwater into the North Atlantic would have had a massive impact on the circulation of the ocean currents. As shown in chapter 2, warm waters from the Caribbean move northward in the Atlantic Ocean and carry their warmth right up into the Arctic Ocean north of Scandinavia (see the illustration on page 12). The influx of cold North American freshwater would have interrupted this important flow and effectively switched off the oceanic circulation system shown in the illustration on page 141. If the northward flow of warm water stopped, the Arctic Ocean would freeze over and cold polar waters could penetrate southward, cooling the Atlantic seaboard. This is probably how the cold stadial was initiated.

This short but severe climatic fluctuation just 10,000 years ago has some important lessons for today. It demonstrates that the uninterrupted flow of currents in the oceans is vital for the maintenance of the climatic balance of the Earth and that sudden changes in climate can occur if that balance is upset. It also shows how easily the balance can be disturbed, and in days when human activities are altering so many global processes, people need to beware. Humans must avoid crossing an environmental threshold that could set in motion considerable and unstoppable changes.

Because of their sensitivity to climatic conditions, glacial movements are thus effective monitors of changing climate. Geologists have spent much effort in recording past movements of glaciers, using various types of evidence, in order to reconstruct the history of glacial movements. Studies of the past glacial limits in the valleys of the Swiss Alps have provided a detailed record of climatic changes over the past 1,000 years. They were in retreat in the 10th to the 13th centuries, the so-called Medieval Warm Period, but then advanced to achieve greater extent in 1385. The glaciers advanced and retreated on various occasions during the 17th century and made their most recent advance around 1860. These glacial advances correspond with many other pieces of evidence for particularly cold conditions at these times, and this part of history, falling between the 14th century and the mid-19th century, has come to be known as the Little Ice Age. But since 1860 the glaciers in the Swiss Alps, together with those of Norway and even the high altitude but low latitude glaciers of the African mountains such as Kilimanjaro, have been in retreat.

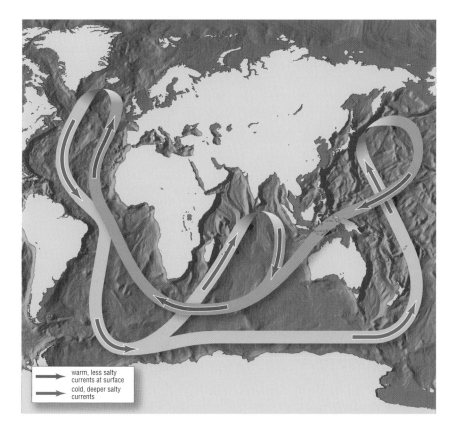

warm, less salty currents at surface

cold, deeper salty currents

*The oceanic conveyor belt that circulates around the world's oceans. Cold, salty water is dense, so it moves along at depth, while warm, less saline water moves at the surface of the ocean.*

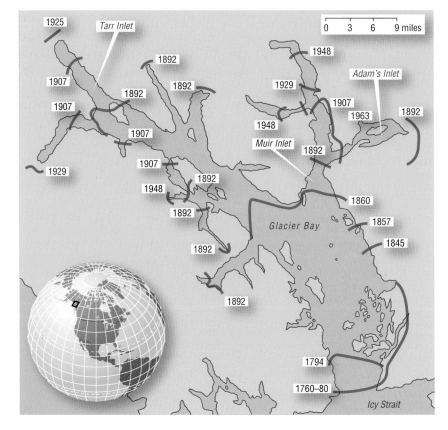

1925
Tarr Inlet
0    3    6    9 miles
1892
1948
Adam's Inlet
1907
1892
1892
1929
1907
1907
1892
1892
1963
1892
1907
1948
Muir Inlet
1929
1892
1907
1860
1948
1892
Glacier Bay
1857
1892
1845
1892
1794
1760–80
Icy Strait

*The northward retreat of ice in Glacier Bay, Alaska, since the 18th century. As the Earth has become warmer, following the Little Ice Age of the 14th to the 19th centuries, glaciers have been retreating around the world.*

One glacier that has been studied in considerable detail is the Jotunheimen in southern Norway, which has retreated by about a mile (1.5 km) in 200 years. Geologists have made even more detailed and long-term observations at the Glacier Bay glacier in Alaska. Its northward retreat has been recorded since the 18th century and the limits of the glacier can be accurately traced (see illustration above). During the 200 years between 1760 and 1960, this glacier withdrew about 45 miles (72 km). Glaciers and their movements are thus proving to be one of the most sensitive indicators of the current global warming.

## Causes of glaciation

Although there have been several episodes of glacial activity in the Earth's history, during which ice caps have been present in the polar regions, these are the exception rather than the rule. For the bulk of the Earth's existence there have been no ice sheets or glaciers, so present-day conditions are by no means typical for the planet. Why the Earth should have periodically entered such a state over the past 2 billion years remains something of a mystery, and observers have put forward various theories to account for the rare instances of glaciation.

The basis of one such theory is incomplete oceanic circulation. One thing that is evidently needed for polar ice caps to develop is the presence of a continental landmass at or near the poles or for the landmasses to be so arranged that the free circulation of waters around the Earth is interrupted. This prevents the redistribution of energy from the Tropics to polar regions. The relative isolation of the Arctic Ocean by the ring of continents that currently surround it, for example, may have played an important part in encouraging the Pleistocene glaciations. Other possible explanations relate to the circulation of the atmosphere. The elevation of mountain ranges, such as the Himalayas and the Tibetan Plateau, can also create new atmospheric circulation patterns that may induce major global climatic changes, as can periods of excessive volcanism. It is interesting to note that the onset of the most recent Ice Age coincided with the elevation of the Alps and the Himalayas. Yet another hypothesis takes into account events in space. Interstellar dust and belts of asteroids could be responsible for periods of poorer penetration of the Sun's energy to the Earth's surface. Clearly ideas abound, but a full explanation of the occasional episodes of glaciation on Earth is still some way off.

Intensive study of the Pleistocene glaciations, however, does provide some information about the pattern of glacial cycles once an ice age has commenced. The last 2 million years have shown a distinct pattern of glacial and interglacial cycles. These have a cycle wavelength of about 100,000 years. As long ago as 1864, Scottish geologists suggested that ice ages could be caused by astronomical factors, particularly the way in which the Earth wobbles on its axis in a regular and predictable way. But it was a Yugoslav physicist, Milutin Milankovitch (1879–1955), who finally put together a full explanation of the cyclic pattern of the glacials during the Pleistocene (see sidebar on page 144).

## The Milankovitch theory

Milutin Milankovitch (1879–1955) proposed the first comprehensive explanation of the cyclic pattern of the glacials observed in the Pleistocene. In essence, Milankovitch claimed that there are three patterns, all superimposed on one another, that cause the observed pattern of glacial and interglacial cycles. First, the Earth follows an elliptical orbit around the Sun, not a circular one. The result is that the Earth is closer to the Sun every 100,000 years. Second, the Earth is not upright on its axis, and the tilt of the Earth varies resulting in stronger seasonal differences in temperature at certain times in history; this fluctuation operates on a cycle of about 40,000 years. Third, there is the wobble of the Earth on its axis, like a spinning top that has hit a bump, which occurs in a cycle of 21,000 years. When these three cycles are combined to create a predicted model of how climate should have changed over the past million years, they form a picture that closely resembles the geological facts.

The expected timing of glacial episodes on the basis of the Milankovitch calculations corresponds quite well with the observed dates obtained from field surveys. There are complications, of course, but basically the astronomical theory devised by Milankovitch forms an excellent basis for explaining glacial patterns. When he first proposed his model in the 1930s, few geologists were impressed, but as more information has accumulated the Milankovitch theory has gained much ground. It is now generally accepted as the major underlying cause of the Pleistocene pattern of glacial and interglacial cycles.

Obviously, many other factors besides astronomical ones influence the pattern of glacials and interglacials, so the astronomical theory must be regarded simply as a starting point in explaining the history of ice on Earth. As already discussed, ocean circulation patterns can change global climate patterns as can mountain building episodes that alter the circulation of the atmosphere. When volcanoes erupt, they eject huge quantities of dust into the atmosphere that can alter the climate of the whole planet. For instance, in 1982 the volcano El Chichón in the Yucatán Peninsula of Mexico forced an estimated 16 million tons of dust into the atmosphere and prevented much solar energy from reaching the Earth's surface. Such dust veils can reduce the Earth's temperature substantially. Major eruptions of volcanoes in 1783 resulted in a temperature decline of 3°F (1.5°C) over the

Northern Hemisphere. So, while the climate of the Earth is what primarily controls the extent of ice on the planet and therefore the distribution of the tundra biome, many other factors can also affect the climate.

## Biological history of tundra

Ice ages, as discussed earlier in this chapter, are relatively rare and widely spaced events in the history of the planet (see table on page 131). Consequently the organisms able to survive in tundra habitats have had an interrupted history. There is very little information about the types of organisms that may have inhabited the tundra regions in the early history of the Earth, in Precambrian times, but presumably they were limited to primitive bacteria. When the polar ice caps returned in Carboniferous times, however, land vegetation was present, and fossils of the cold regions have survived.

At this time, some 300 million years ago, many of the present-day continents were all joined together in massive supercontinents. North America and Europe lay together, forming the supercontinent of Laurasia. They had recently become separated from another, and larger, landmass to their south. This southern landmass, called Gondwana, consisted of what are now South America, Africa, Antarctica, India, and Australia, and it lay over the South Pole. Perhaps the location of this huge landmass over a polar position accounts for the development of an ice age. In any event, an ice sheet formed over what is now Antarctica and spread out over the rest of Gondwana. Laurasia lay over the equator; its climate, therefore, was a hot tropical one, and the extensive swamp forests that formed at this time became the great deposits of coal buried within North America and Europe.

While the equatorial supercontinent of Laurasia was occupied by peat-forming swamps, the conditions on Gondwana, to the south, were very different. In the northern part of Gondwana (what is now northern South America and Africa) was a dry desert. But farther south, around the ice sheet, conditions were much cooler and the region bore very different vegetation. Woody shrubs grew here, particularly a plant called *Glossopteris,* which has given its name to an entire vegetation type, the *Glossopteris* flora. These plants belong to an extinct group called seed ferns. Their leaves looked like ferns and they were long regarded as true ferns until fossils were found that showed they bore seeds. They are now believed to be more closely related to the conifers. The wood of these plants from the permafrost regions of the Gondwana tundra shows distinct series of rings, indicating a strong seasonality of growth (unlike the plants of the tropical coal swamps, which had no discernible growth rings). Being quite close to the South Pole, the *Glossopteris* shrubs must have survived through long polar nights in which little or no growth was possible and then grown vigorously when the summer season arrived. What is remarkable is the size of these woody plants, considering how close to the South Pole they grew. The Carboniferous/Permian Ice Age of about 300 million to 280 million years ago included at least five cycles of glacial advance and retreat. The *Glossopteris* flora represents the first known tundra vegetation on Earth. As conditions became warmer in Permian times, and the Earth emerged from that ice age, the *Glossopteris* flora gradually disappeared, presumably evolving new forms in response to the changed set of conditions or giving way to other plant types that were better equipped to cope with the changes, such as *Dicroidium,* another seed fern.

After the Permian, when the first tundra vegetation died out, Earth's climate did not enter another ice age for a long time. There is some evidence for glaciation in what is now Antarctica in Jurassic times, 150 million years ago, but it was not extensive. A different story emerges around 32 million years ago, when the Antarctic Ice Sheet began to form once again. The climate of the Earth was evidently on a gentle cooling trend and glaciation commenced on high mountains in Alaska by about 12 million years ago. This was when the tundra plants and animals known today must have begun their evolution. This tundra, therefore, is the youngest of all the Earth's natural biomes. For many millions of years there had been no equivalent habitat on Earth—and this is true of no other biome. There have been tropical forests, temperate forests, open scrub, and deserts of one type or another throughout the history of the planet, at least since land plants and animals first evolved. But the history of this recent tundra has been repeatedly interrupted, and each time an ice age has hit the Earth, the plants and animals have had to begin over again in their adaptation to the new environment.

In the recent ice age (the last 10 million years), the likely origins of plants and animals appropriate to tundra conditions are the mountains and the coniferous forests. The high mountains of the world, such as those of Alaska 12 million years ago, were becoming colder, subjecting the natural vegetation to increasing stress. Forests had occupied even the high mountains in Miocene times, but conditions must have made tree growth increasingly difficult, producing a more open canopy. The increased light penetration would have led to the evolution of new forms in the ground vegetation. Plants of the blueberry family (Ericaceae), the saxifrages (Saxifragaceae), the pinks (Caryophyllaceae), the cress family (Brassicaceae), the grasses (Poaceae), the rushes (Juncaceae), and the poppies (Papaveraceae) were all important in the founding of tundra vegetation. Plants of wetlands, especially the sedges (Cyperaceae), also found conditions in the developing tundra suitable for their needs. Among the trees, birches (Betulaceae) and willows (Salicaceae) proved most able to develop new forms that could cope with cold and wind exposure. Joining them, of course, were the mosses and lichens that could survive even under the harshest conditions. Most important among these were the bog mosses (*Sphagnum* species) and the "reindeer moss" group of lichens (*Cladonia* species).

Many mammals evolved tundra forms, among them some surprising groups. The bears proved adaptable, as did deer (such as caribou), the elephants (mammoths and mastodons), foxes, cats, rodents, and especially the mustelids (including stoats, weasels, and wolverines). Birds adapted to fit the conditions, including songbirds (such as buntings), owls, raptors (such as falcons and eagles), and grouse, together with a wide range of seabirds and waders. As the tundra habitats developed and extended, some mammals and birds developed migratory patterns, allowing them to exploit the productivity of the tundra without having to experience the hardship of polar winters.

Alpine tundra on the lower-latitude mountains also developed as the world grew cooler. Many of the plants and animals that were adapting to the polar conditions also succeeded in the mountains, but their geographical isolation produced some differences. Mountaintops are rather like islands in the ocean. They can be widely separated from one another and the intervening landscape can be difficult to cross. As a result many mountains began to develop their own plants and animals in isolation from the general evolution of tundra organisms. Many alpine species, unable to interbreed with other members of their groups on neighboring mountains because of the difficulties of travel, began to evolve separately and produce new forms. The East African mountains (see "Tundra plants," pages 86–94) are an excellent example of this process, in which strange and unique forms arose. Species that have developed in and remain restricted to their geographical ranges in this way are called *endemics*. Mountain tundra is a habitat rich in endemic species, which makes them important as reserves of the world's biodiversity.

## People in the tundra

The human species, *Homo sapiens,* first appeared during the Pleistocene and is likely to have originated in Africa. Genetic evidence suggests that all modern humans have a common ancestor. Humans proved very adaptable to the changing climate; modifying the environment by wearing the skins of animals and living in caves heated by fire meant that humans were able to cope with cooler climates, even the extremes of the tundra. During the last ice age, humans occupied much of Europe and Asia, hunting many of the large herbivores of the tundra. In what is now Russia, people preyed heavily on mammoths and even used their bones to construct dwellings. Cave-dwelling people in the west of Europe painted pictures of their prey animals on the walls of their caves, perhaps hoping thereby to obtain some magical power over them in the chase. They used primitive weapons of stone, but by hunting in packs and driving game into confined spaces or traps or over cliffs, they were able to achieve much more than might have been expected of such a relatively small predator. They also domesticated the wolf and used this animal as an assistant in driving game.

Late in the last glaciation (probably before the maximum glacial advance 20,000 years ago), humans crossed from Asia into North America. World sea levels were low at that time, so the narrow seas that separate Alaska from Russia were then mainly dry land, offering no serious barrier to the movement of animals, including humans. From these invading people the whole of the Americas was populated, possibly in several waves. A study of the ancient languages of the Native North American populations suggests that there were three main groups: one centered in the far north and west, one on the Pacific coast, and one in the larger southern region of what is now the United States. These were the areas that were not covered by ice during the final (Wisconsin) glaciation, and the Stone Age peoples occupying these tundra landscapes around the edge of the massive ice sheet probably survived by hunting the tundra animals.

The impact of hunters upon these animals, especially the very large ones such as mammoths, proved fatal. All over the world, within a few thousand years of human settlement, the great mammals or "megafauna" of the tundra were all extinct, including mastodon, cave bear, giant elk, and mammoth (see sidebar on page 150). The debate about these extinctions, and the role of humans in causing them, is still not finally settled, but many pieces of evidence point to a human agent. The timing of the extinctions is remarkably consistent, occurring largely between 12,000 and 10,500 years ago. This was when human populations were growing and people were developing more sophisticated stone weapons. Climate, however, was also changing rapidly at this time. Could the loss of these large tundra animals have been due to the reduced area of tundra habitat? Certainly this would have constrained their populations, but several other warm interglacial periods during the past 2 million years had occurred that had not proved fatal to these species, so what was different about this one? The answer seems to be humans. Never before had the large mammals faced such a formidable predator. For these cumbersome beasts, which were becoming increasingly restricted in their

## The woolly mammoth

The woolly mammoth had the appearance of an elephant with long, shaggy hair. It stood about 13 feet (4 m) high at the shoulder and its tusks could grow to a length of about 15 feet (4.5 m). These tusks can still be found buried in the soils of the tundra regions, especially in Siberia, where local people have made an income by selling them to ivory traders. It was one such seeker of ivory who first discovered an intact body of a woolly mammoth embedded in permafrost in 1799. It was extracted relatively intact and studied by scientists.

Since then many such bodies have come to light and the possibility has been discussed that the DNA could be used to reconstruct the species, possibly using the elephant as a surrogate mother. These "Jurassic Park" plans, however, have not yet proved viable because DNA is a relatively fragile molecule, and even when preserved in ice it has usually severely degenerated over the course of many thousands of years.

area of occupation as the tundra retreated, human presence was the final nail in their coffin.

The Inuit people of the Arctic regions (one of the three North American language groups) settled the northern regions of what is now Canada in prehistoric times. They spread from Alaska, where they arrived after crossing the Bering land bridge from Russia, and gradually extended their range eastward, reaching Ellesmere Island to the west of Greenland about 4,000 years ago. Using ice as their winter building material and skins and bark in summer, they left little evidence of their occupation for archaeologists to study. But more permanent settlements, such as campsites that used boulders in protective circles, still survive and supply evidence of a way of life that must have changed little over many thousands of years. Ellesmere Island lies only 470 miles (756 km) from the North Pole, so the prehistoric people who occupied the region must have been extremely hardy to persist in the face of the extremely harsh climate. Like the modern Inuit peoples, they would have subsisted largely on animal flesh obtained by hunting. Seals, birds, caribou, and fish probably formed the major part of their diet.

The Viking, or Norse, people of Scandinavia were great travelers and colonists, and they spread out across the islands of the North Atlantic around the 10th century C.E. They settled Iceland and southern Greenland, surviving there for several centuries. Dispute still surrounds the claim that they traveled farther and even reached North America. One of their traditional tales, or sagas, tells of the land of Vinland, where the wild grape was discovered. Archaeological evidence indicates that they settled Newfoundland, but penetration farther south cannot be conclusively proved.

Antarctica essentially has no prehistory. People did not reach this continent—or, indeed, confirm its existence—until the late 15th century. It is the one continent that has a history devoid of the impact of humankind until very recent times.

Although archaeologists know something of the people of the Arctic tundra during prehistoric times, until very recently they knew next to nothing of human activities in the alpine tundra regions. The high mountains of the world

*Inuit hunters with their harvest of caribou carcasses in Alaska. Caribou have long been an important prey item for the Inuit people. (Photo by Michio Hoshino/Minden Pictures)*

seemed, like Antarctica, to be devoid of prehistoric human life. In September 1991, however, two German mountaineers were climbing in the Italian Tyrol district of the Alps in Europe. They were descending from a mountain peak they had climbed close to the Italian/Austrian border and were crossing an ice field when they saw something brown sticking out of the ice. It was the head and shoulders of a dead body emerging from melting ice. Assuming that it was an unfortunate mountaineer who had met with a recent accident, they reported it to the police in Austria where they descended. When the body was recovered and examined by pathologists and archaeologists, it proved to be the victim of a very old mountaineering accident, not a recent one. In fact, the body was about 5,000 years old and had been preserved in the ice ever since the unfortunate traveler had perished, probably in a snowstorm while crossing from Austria to Italy. He wore clothing made of chamois skins, padded with grass to increase the thermal insulation. His boots were also filled with grass, and he wore a bearskin hat. He carried a bow and a quiver full of arrows, so he was either a huntsman or was expecting trouble on his journey. He also had equipment for lighting a fire and an ice ax made of copper. Forensic scientists who analyzed the DNA in samples from his body confirmed that he had originated from north-central Europe. It seems he was either crossing into Italy or was on the return journey to his northern home.

This discovery in the Alps has provided a rare, if not unique, glimpse into the life of prehistoric humans in the alpine tundra regions. There is much archaeological evidence for settlements in the Alpine valleys, where ancient people farmed. They apparently needed to cross the high mountains on their travels and they may have also used the high pastures and alpine tundra for grazing animals in summer. These prehistoric people were familiar with the changeable and dangerous weather of the mountains and had developed equipment to cope with these conditions. The fact that so few bodies have been found suggests that they coped fairly well in lands that presented so many survival problems.

## Tundra exploration

The tundra regions of the Arctic, then, were inhabited by people long before the world's civilizations were fully aware of the existence and geography of such lands. The northern lands were largely known through vague myths and stories. Global exploration, until very recent times, was driven mainly by the need to expand the opportunities for food production to support human populations, or to gain wealth through trade, so the far north had few attractions. The Viking people of Scandinavia were the only European culture to exploit the economic opportunity of colonizing the remote North Atlantic islands and seaboards. The discovery (or perhaps more accurately, the rediscovery) of North America by Christopher Columbus (1451–1506) in 1492 came at a time when global travel and trade by sea were increasing rapidly. European colonialism became an incentive for further exploration that lasted for several centuries and led, among other things, to the first modern expeditions by Europeans into the far north. Most such voyages of discovery proved disastrous, but explorers made enormous efforts to discover a northwest passage that would link the North Atlantic to the North Pacific. If found, it would provide a trade route to the Far East, allowing ships to avoid the lengthy and dangerous passage around Cape Horn at the southern tip of South America or eastward around the Cape of Good Hope in South Africa.

Exploration in the Arctic in search of the Northwest Passage accelerated in the 18th century, and many lost their lives in trying to win the prizes European governments offered to anyone who found it. Most expeditions set off from the Atlantic and many ended in Hudson Bay, but at the end of the 18th century attention moved to the North Pacific. The British naval officer George Vancouver (1757–98) took his ship, HMS *Discovery,* into the Icy Strait of Glacier Bay in Alaska in 1794 and was impressed by the 10-mile-long (16-km) ice wall where glaciers entered the ocean (see the illustration on page 142). The American naturalist and conservationist John Muir (1838–1914) visited the region 85 years later and found that the glaciers had retreated 48 miles (77 km), probably as a consequence of global warming. The main glacier of Glacier Bay subsequently became known as the Muir Glacier.

Exploration of the northern regions also proceeded on land, particularly by companies interested in fur trading. In 1789 the Scot Alexander Mackenzie (1755–1850), who was employed by the North West Fur Company, set out with Native American and Canadian colleagues in birch-bark canoes to seek a river route from the continental areas of North America into the North Pacific. He found a great river that led westward from the Great Slave Lake, but it gradually turned northward and eventually led into the Arctic Ocean instead of the Pacific. He named it the "River of Disappointment," but it later became known as the Mackenzie River. The expedition may not have discovered a link to the West Coast, but it did represent a major advance in the exploration of the tundra regions. The discovery also opened up the region to fur trappers, whale hunters, and gold prospectors. It is now an important region for oil extraction.

The 19th century saw a great rise in public interest in exploration in general, and the inaccessible tundra regions of the world rivaled the inaccessible center of Africa in its attractions for the intrepid explorer. The romantic image of the far north, with its mountainous icebergs and bleak isolation, was stimulated to some extent by the publication of Mary Shelley's novel *Frankenstein* in 1818, which depicted its now-famous monster in the icy tundra setting. The British launched a series of expeditions to try to reach the North Pole during the early part of the 19th century, but they all became stranded in sea ice, having to either turn back their ships or abandon land-based excursions over the ice. The British were determined to discover a northwest passage to the Pacific, their interests being more economic and competitive (beating the Russians to the discovery) than scientific. Perhaps the best known of these remarkably brave explorers is John Ross (1800–62), whose name now identifies several geographical and biological features, including Ross's gull and Ross's goose. The first European to spend a winter in the High Arctic (in 1820) was William Edward Parry (1790–1855), who wrote of the "deathlike stillness" and the "dreary desolation" of the experience.

In the late 19th century the media entered into the realm of exploration. James Gordon Bennett, Jr. (1841–1918), editor of the *New York Herald* newspaper, was a great supporter of exploration. His most famous exploit was to support Henry Morton Stanley (1841–1904) in his search for Dr. David Livingstone (1813–73) in remotest Africa, but he also sponsored Arctic exploration. In July 1879 he provided the financial backing for an attempt to reach the North Pole by George Washington De Long (1844–81). Believing that the North Pole was surrounded by open ocean, De Long set out northward from the Bering Strait, but by September his boat encountered masses of pack ice, and he spent two years in the Arctic Ocean north of Siberia before the boat was eventually frozen in and crushed. Three open boats set off from the wreck. Only one of the boats reached safety; De Long and his party died before help could reach them.

The successful discovery of the Northwest Passage did not occur until the voyage of Roald Amundsen (1872–1928), a Norwegian who later became the first man to reach the South Pole. His voyage took place between 1903 and 1906 and it took him north of Baffin Island and Hudson Bay, through Baffin Bay, and then through the channels separating Victoria Island and Banks Island from the mainland. Eventually Amundsen arrived at the Mackenzie River delta. To travel from there to the Bering Strait, he had to wait until the ice had melted, and then he finally sailed down the West Coast to San Francisco. By the time he arrived, the news of his success had already become a little stale. Moreover, the excitement that might once have surrounded the achievement had diminished: Although the existence of the route had now been demonstrated, it clearly could never become commercially important. (Flight has changed this. Perhaps ironically, jets from Europe to the west coast of North America essentially follow the course of the long-hoped-for Northwest Passage through the Arctic tundra.)

The North Pole itself eluded human contact until April 1909, when a U.S. naval officer, Robert Edwin Peary (1856–1920), led an expedition from Fort Conger on Ellesmere Island in Canada. Using relays of dogsleds and aided by the Inuit people, the team laid out a route with supply stations.

Peary himself, together with one companion, covered the final 155 miles (250 km). The achievement was marred to some extent by a claim (that later proved false) by another explorer that he had reached the North Pole in the previous year. But Peary and his companion are now regarded as the first people ever to reach this remote and ice-bound location. The seasonal timing of such expeditions is critical, since they must take place after the worst of the winter weather and yet before the Arctic Ocean pack ice breaks up and becomes dangerous. Besides the dangers of collapsing or rafting ice, there is the ever-present risk of wandering polar bears who can prove aggressive.

People had long been aware of the existence of the Arctic tundra. The Vikings were familiar with the tundra, and tales of the bleak north were present in Greek and Roman mythology, which suggests that even these early civilizations had some contact with the far north. The Antarctic, however, was shrouded in mystery until very recent times. The Greek philosopher and naturalist Aristotle speculated in the fourth century B.C.E. that the great northern landmasses must be "balanced" by a landmass in the deep south. This supposed continent later became known as Terra Australis Incognita, the "Unknown Southern Land." Aristotle called it "Antarktikos." The northern lands lay under the constellation Arktos, "The Bear," so the southern lands must be the opposite of this, he reasoned.

When the Portuguese explorer Vasco da Gama (1469–1525) sailed around the southern tip of Africa and eventually reached India in 1497, he proved that Africa was not joined to the Unknown Southern Land. Ferdinand Magellan (1480–1521), another native of Portugal, sought the southern tip of South America in 1519. He sailed through the straits that now bear his name, which separate the mainland of South America and the island of Tierra del Fuego to its south. But he was not sure whether this was truly an island or another great landmass, the Unknown Southern Land. The English sailor Francis Drake (1540–96) settled this issue when his ship was blown south in the Pacific by a great storm and ended up rounding Cape Horn, thus demonstrating that there was no connection between South America and the

Southern Land. He also provided the first description of penguins, noting that they were easy to catch (being flightless) and good to eat.

By the mid-17th century, Dutch traders were regularly sailing in the South Pacific, traveling along the west coast of Australia, and they considered it possible that this was the Unknown Southern Land of Aristotle. Among these Dutch explorers, Abel Janszoon Tasman (1603–59) was the first to circumnavigate Australia and to encounter Tasmania and New Zealand. But these lands were temperate in latitude and climate, not the equivalent of the Arctic wastes.

The notion that the Antarctic continent might exist continued to appeal to explorers, but it did not have the economic appeal of the Arctic in terms of the new sea routes it might possibly offer. The fishing and whaling potential of the Southern Ocean, however, eventually led to its systematic exploration. The British navigator James Cook (1728–79) spent much of his time exploring the Pacific Ocean, including its southern regions, during the latter half of the 18th century. He was the first to sail south of the Antarctic Circle, in 1773, but had to turn back on his southbound voyage because of pack ice. He little realized that he was only 80 miles (130 km) from the legendary continent. Cook succeeded in circumnavigating the fringing ice packs of Antarctica but was never convinced that the southern polar regions contained more than floating ice.

It was a Russian, Fabian Gottlieb von Bellingshausen (1778–1852), who first sighted land in 1820. In unusual conditions of excellent visibility (something denied to Cook), he spotted high cliffs of rock, thus proving that a southern continent existed. The first person to set foot on the continent was John Davis, an American sailor, who landed on the Antarctic Peninsula (see the map on page 3) just a year later, in 1821. James Ross, of Arctic tundra fame, was also eager to add the Antarctic to his polar explorations, and in 1841 he led an expedition that aimed to reach the South Pole. As he approached the Pole, however, he found his passage blocked by an enormous mass of pack ice, now known as the Ross Ice Shelf, and he was unable even to approach the region of Antarctica in which the Pole lies. He did, however, see a great volcano that was active at that time, and he named it Mount Erebus. *Erebus* is the name the Greeks gave to the region of darkness through which the dead must pass, which gives some indication of the awe in which Ross and his fellow sailors held these inhospitable regions. The volcano remains periodically active, but its main claim to fame is a tragic accident in 1979, when a plane carrying tourists became enveloped in a blizzard and crashed on its slopes, killing 257 passengers and crew.

The South Pole itself was not reached until 1911, as a result of a dramatic and tragic race between two teams of explorers. From Norway came a team led by Roald Amundsen, and from Britain, one led by Robert Scott (1868–1912). The Norwegians set out on October 19, using four sledges pulled by dogs. Their most difficult section consisted of the climb up to the polar plateau, over the dangerous ice mass of the Axel Heiberg Glacier. From there, the going became easier as Amundsen's team crossed the relatively flat plateau, eventually reaching the South Pole on December 14 and raising the Norwegian flag. The British team reached the Pole on January 17, having hauled their sledges over the entire course, without the use of dogs. Scott's comment on reaching the South Pole was, "This is a terrible place." Ill fortune plagued the return journey of Scott's team. Despite acts of heroism and self-sacrifice, blizzards and frostbite took the lives of all members before they could reach their base. Once again, the remarkable success of Roald Amundsen was somewhat overshadowed in the news media by the romantic yet tragic failure of Scott's team. In both his Northwest Passage expedition and in his attainment of the South Pole, Amundsen seems to have missed out on the public acclaim that was his due.

With the Amundsen and Scott expeditions the great romantic age of Antarctic exploration ended and the period of commercial and scientific investigation took over. This was also the beginning of a period of human history in which the human population has expanded dramatically and the need for food and raw materials has led people to exploit even the most unlikely of the world's wildernesses. Having discovered the vastness of the tundra in general and

Antarctica in particular, humanity now asked how the tundra could be used to human advantage.

## Conclusions

Ice ages, periods when ice sheets and tundra are present on Earth, are relatively rare events in the history of the planet and seem to occur in a regular pattern, roughly every 150 million years. The causes of these long-term climate cycles are not understood, but the events may relate to the positions of continents on the surface of the Earth and the way they influence ocean currents. Earth is currently occupying a warm interval within an ice age, and it is possible to detect more detailed patterns of climatic fluctuation, with alternating peaks of warmth and cold at intervals of approximately 100,000 years. This scale of climate pattern appears to be related to astronomical factors, especially the varying distance between the Earth and the Sun.

Tundra plants and animals have also experienced an interrupted history, and the present vegetation and fauna of tundra is relatively recent in origin, perhaps less than 10 million years old. High mountain organisms may well have been the first tundra dwellers, expanding in range and abundance as the cold of the current Ice Age intensified, especially over the past million years.

Humans lived in tundra habitats of Europe and Asia throughout the last glacial period, which reached its maximum extent around 20,000 years ago. They spread from the eastern tip of Asia into North America as that glacial episode began to recede, passing over what was then a dry land bridge between Asia and Alaska. The Inuit people took up permanent residence in the tundra and adapted their culture to life in the bitter cold of the far north. Viking exploration around the 10th century C.E. led to the invasion of European peoples into the North Atlantic tundra regions, but these settlements proved to be temporary. Renewed exploration began in the 15th century when commercial traders sought alternative routes to the Far East, and this led to a fuller understanding of the geography and biology of the Arctic tundra.

The Antarctic has never been populated, even in prehistory. The existence of a great southern continent was hypothesized since classical times, but evidence was lacking until the intrepid sea voyages of the 18th and early 19th century. The first human to reach the South Pole, the Norwegian Roald Amundsen, achieved this goal only in 1911, less than a century ago. Human history in the Antarctic, therefore, is very recent and brief.

# CHAPTER 6

# USES OF THE TUNDRA

Whenever people have discovered and explored a new region of the world, their first concern has been its exploitation. The hope of becoming rich has often motivated those setting up exploratory expeditions, even though the geographers and biologists involved in them may have had higher and more scientific aims. The tundra regions of the world are no exception, and many of the early expeditions into the Arctic were concerned with the discovery of new trade routes that would bring faster travel and greater riches. Once these hopes were abandoned, the potential of the Arctic wilderness for hunting and mineral prospecting soon took over. Understanding the economic value of the tundra helps us to appreciate its history and also provides an insight into the problems that this biome will face in the future.

## Hunting and trapping

Hunting has been the basis of human life in the tundra since the human species first invaded this realm. Tundra plant life offers few opportunities for food gathering, apart from some berries in the late summer. Agriculture, as the Norse people invading Iceland and Greenland were to discover, was of little use in these northern latitudes. But herds of large grazing mammals, such as mammoths and caribou, provided a reliable source of food for human cultures prepared for a largely carnivorous diet. The Inuit people of Alaska and northern Canada have traditionally been coastal in their distribution and marine-based in their culture. The most northerly settlement of people in North America is on Ellesmere Island, where Inuit settlers have been present for at least 4,000 years.

Later, when European explorers and pioneers penetrated north through the boreal forests of Canada, they discovered lands rich in mammals whose skins were extremely valuable in the fashionable cities of the south. Similarly, the wastes of Siberia provided a supply of furs for the citizens of Moscow and St. Petersburg in Russia, so trappers lived hard lives but made good profits. Trading companies such as the Hudson's Bay Company developed more formal routes for the movement of furs from the outback to the consumers in the cities. For many decades, the wealth of the tundra lands, north of the forests, lay mainly in their mammals.

In Europe one animal, the caribou or reindeer, formed the main source of sustenance for the Sami (sometimes called Lapp) people of northern Scandinavia. They followed the migratory herds over the tundra landscape, using the animals as a source of meat and hides. They protected the herds from other predators, such as wolves, thus ensuring that young calves survived and increased the size of the herds. Thus began a kind of symbiotic relationship between the Sami people and the reindeer, resulting in a partial domestication of this docile mammal. Herds are now carefully protected and managed in northern Europe and Asia and remain the foundation on which Sami culture is based.

In Antarctica, uncontrolled hunting of marine mammals for their skins became a major industry within a few decades of Captain Cook's first penetration of the Antarctic Circle in 1773 (see "Tundra exploration," pages 153–159). Seals, including fur seals, were abundant in the sub-Antarctic islands at the beginning of the 19th century, but many of these island colonies had been completely exterminated by 1830. When the seal populations had been depleted, hunters turned to penguins, which provided a source of oil from their stored fat. Protection of seals and penguins in recent times has fortunately led to the recovery of many species, including fur seals and king penguins.

Whales abounded in the southern oceans, and whaling stations were set up in the early 20th century on the Antarctic islands to assist in the harvesting and butchering of these enormous marine mammals. The major impact on whale populations began with the development of sophisticated hunting methods, powerful harpoons, and robust ships. The major problem with whale harvesting is the animals' very slow rate of reproduction, which means that populations recover from losses very slowly. Since 1949 the International Whaling Commission has attempted to regulate whale harvesting and since the 1960s some species have been fully protected. Some whale species are now increasing their populations, but whales have slow breeding rates, so it will take a long time for these animals to recover fully from the impact of hunting.

Native peoples of the Arctic regions have a long history of hunting seals and cetaceans (whales and dolphins). For many species, hunting by traditional methods involves a limited harvest that is sustainable. In the case of the beluga, for example, a regulated harvest is possible. But for some scarcer species, such as the bowhead whale, the largest of the Arctic sea mammals, even a small harvest could damage the limited population. This means that even the traditional hunting by native tundra peoples needs to be monitored and controlled. Seal hunting for skins that can be exported, which has traditionally played an important part in the economy of the Inuit people, has suffered a major downturn in recent years. The reason is that the demand for seal skins around the world has declined as people have moved from animal skin to synthetic materials for their clothing. Ecological concerns among the consumers of the world are having a substantial impact on the economy of the people of the far north.

Hunting in alpine tundra has also resulted in drastic falls in the populations of some mammals. Bighorn sheep have suffered in North America, and chamois and ibex have undergone considerable declines in the Alps of Europe. All of these species have increased as a result of protection in recent years. Hunting is still permitted, but it is controlled and is often directed at the large males that are prized as trophies. Even this activity, however, could have an impact on the genetic constitution of the species because it involves the consistent elimination of the biggest and perhaps the fittest males.

## Mineral reserves

Mineral prospecting in the tundra regions developed alongside hunting and trapping in the early history of tundra exploitation. In the early days, the remoteness and the transport difficulties meant that only the most valuable of geological resources were worth pursuing, and chief among these was gold.

On July 17, 1897, a steamship arrived in Seattle harbor from the extreme northwest of Canada. It carried news of a considerable strike of gold on the Klondike River, a tributary of the Yukon River of Alaska. The news became exaggerated when journalists claimed that the boat contained a ton of solid gold, and the outcome was a crazed rush into the northern lands of men lured by the prospect of untold riches. The strike was indeed a rich one, but the Klondike River lay in an extremely remote region of mountains, and those who set off faced extreme hardships of travel and survival in the inhospitable tundra. Nevertheless, prospectors arrived not only from North America but also from as far as Europe and Australia, and the settlement of Dawson City soon became a boomtown to service the gold rush of the Klondike.

The extraction of mineral wealth inevitably involves geological disturbance and results in the contamination and silting of streams and rivers. This was not a primary concern in the late 19th century, but it has become an increasingly important consideration in the environmentally conscious days of the 21st century. A modern understanding of the fragility of the tundra ecosystem has added to these concerns. Although the extraction of gold from rocks is now more sophisticated and efficient than in the days of the Klondike gold rush, the efficiency of extraction means that larger masses of rock can be treated and more waste is produced. Extraction of enough gold for a pair of wedding bands can generate a truckload of waste rock. The environmental damage associated with gold mining, however, has now moved from the tundra regions to the Tropics, in Brazil and Africa.

The tundra habitats of high mountains are also subject to mining activities. The mountains of Utah contain the largest hole that has ever been created by human mining activities, Bingham Canyon. More than 2.5 miles (4 km) in diameter and half a mile (0.8 km) deep, it was created to permit copper extraction from the rocks. Open-pit and strip-mining activities of this type create the most visually destructive impacts on the landscape, but even subsurface mining creates the problem of waste disposal and results in the accumulation of heaps of discarded rock. These piles are often slow to be colonized by plants because of the rock's high metal content. Colonization in the cold tundra habitats is even slower than that associated with lowland spoil heaps. Apart from metals, some mountain areas are mined for the rock itself, which is used for building or decorative purposes. Granite, limestone, and slate are particularly in demand.

The possibility of commercial mineral exploitation in Antarctica has raised many difficult questions about the management of this wilderness continent. In 1959 all interested governments, including the United States and the Soviet Union, signed the Antarctic Treaty. Its main concern was that the continent should be used only for peaceful purposes and scientific research, denying any country the right to establish military bases or to conduct weapons testing on the continent. But environmental protection required more than this, and the question arose of whether and how to exploit the likely mineral resources of Antarctica, a subject not covered by the treaty. During the cold war the Antarctic provided an important point of contact for the great world powers, and the Antarctic Treaty System evolved, which sought to develop international cooperation on management strategies for Antarctica. The signatories of the Antarctic Treaty worked through the 1980s to establish the Convention on the Regulation of Antarctic Mineral Resource Activities, which assumed that mining would occur but tried to keep environmental damage to a minimum. Then, in 1989, France and Australia took a tougher stand and demanded a ban on mining activities. The other nations involved eventually agreed to this policy, but only on the condition that the ban should have a time limit permitting future reconsideration of the use of the mineral resources of Antarctica. The date agreed upon was 2048, a mere 50 years after the agreement came into force. For the present the Antarctic is safe from mineral extraction, but the battle for the protection of the tundra is not completely over. The global demand for mineral resources continues to grow, so there will undoubtedly be renewed pressures upon the Antarctic wilderness by the middle of the 21st century.

In the northern tundra regions, a new resource has been discovered that is creating even greater environmental problems than the gold of the past, namely oil and gas reserves. Major consumers of oil, in particular the United States, have been eager to discover resources within their own national boundaries and thereby to avoid the expense and the vulnerability associated with depending on imports. The tundra regions of Alaska and Canada contain important reserves of oil that are now being extracted. Other reserves will undoubtedly be discovered. It is important to bear in mind, however, that these reserves are limited and will be exhausted relatively quickly. The North Slope of Alaska, for example, is estimated to contain only enough oil to supply all of the demands of the United States for three years. There are major oil fields beneath the Beaufort Sea, along the coastal region of northeastern Alaska and northern Canada. But this region of Alaska comprises the Arctic National Wildlife Refuge, so the goals of providing the nation's energy needs and conserving its wildlife heritage are in conflict. It remains to be seen whether the two goals can coexist. Meanwhile, additional fields are being discovered out among the islands of the Canadian Arctic, so the debate and the problem will continue for some time to come. Global warming and the continued melting of the ice cover in the Arctic Ocean should permit continued exploration of the region (see "Consequences of climate change," pages 175–178).

The exploitation of oil reserves in the tundra lays it open to many harmful environmental impacts. The most obvious of these is spillage and pollution, both at the point of extraction and during transportation. Oil is particularly harmful in marine situations. Having a low density it floats upon water, and, depending on its viscosity and stickiness, it can produce either masses of thick, coagulated rafts or a thin film distributed over a large area. Floating oil is especially harmful to seabirds, because it can coat their feathers and leave them unable to fly or to dive, so oil-contaminated birds are in danger of starvation. In addition, as they preen their feathers the seabirds ingest toxic chemicals from the oil and become poisoned. The oil may also wash onto shores, where it damages marine life along cliffs and beaches. Cleaning up after oil spills usually involves the use of detergents that emulsify the oil, dispersing it into very small globules that eventually decompose in the water. But the detergents are often more harmful to wildlife than the oil itself, and many conservationists believe that the cleaning operations do more damage than good.

Oil extraction in the tundra also involves the establishment of settlements and the development of roads or other transport systems. Settlements generate waste and, as has been described, waste matter decomposition is slow in the tundra, so waste mountains can develop. Apart from being unsightly, waste heaps attract pests, from rats and gulls to polar bears. Road development on tundra soils is also difficult because of the freezing and thawing that takes place each fall and spring. Hard surfaces in the winter turn into wetlands in the summer, and roads quickly break up under the strain. Oil pipelines provide an alternative to the use of truck transport, especially where long distances are involved. The Trans-Alaska Pipeline runs from Prudhoe Bay on the North Slope south to the Gulf of Alaska and avoids the need for

*The Alaska oil pipeline between Prudhoe Bay and the port of Valdez, is owned by Alyeska Company. It crosses the Brooks Range of mountains, North Slope, and heads south toward the Gulf of Alaska.* (Photo by Yva Momatiuk and John Eastcott/ Minden Pictures)

either fleets of tankers to pass through the Bering Strait or lines of trucks to traverse the Alaskan wilderness, but the pipeline nonetheless presents certain problems. Pipelines fragment the landscape and can create barriers to the movement of large mammals, such as migratory caribou. This fragmentation could affect the survival of some herds, isolating them genetically and perhaps exposing them to new levels of predation.

## Ecotourism and recreation

Television, books, and films have provided a wealth of information about the Earth and its wildlife, making the wonders of the natural world more accessible, even those wilderness regions remote from human habitation. It is perhaps inevitable that people increasingly desire to visit such places and experience the wilderness firsthand. As wealth, leisure time, and the availability of global transport increase, more and more people are indulging in an activity that has become known as *ecotourism* (see sidebar at right).

In the late 19th century, the prospect of visiting the Arctic tundra as a tourist was almost as ambitious as space tourism is today. But in 1892 a German shipping company began running tourist trips to the Arctic island of Spitsbergen. Interrupted only by two world wars, these and similar tourist voyages continued until 1975, when an airport was opened on the island. Cruise ships remain the most popular means of visiting the polar regions of both Russia and North America, but the services now provided usually include educational information supplied by expert lecturers and guides. The North Atlantic provides the best opportunities for approaching the polar regions, concentrating on Greenland, Spitsbergen, and Baffin Island in Canada. Voyages in the North Pacific usually focus on Alaska, particularly Glacier Bay, but some trips pass north through the Bering Strait. In recent years, Russian, Canadian, and American icebreakers have even succeeded in taking paying passengers to the North Pole.

One great advantage of using cruise ships as a means of ecotourism is that they can carry in all the supplies needed

## What is ecotourism?

Essentially, ecotourism has two distinct features. First, it is a type of tourism in which the focus of attention and interest is the natural world and its associated human cultures. Ecotourists seek out wilderness areas of natural beauty in order to appreciate the scenic wonders, exciting wildlife, and distinctive culture of the resident people. Second, ecotourism sets out to be environmentally friendly, seeking to avoid any ecological damage to the area visited: to look but not touch. In some respects ecotourism has replaced the game-hunting of former times. The gun has been replaced by the camera, and the hunting no longer results in the death of an animal.

The desire to avoid any harmful impact, however, is very difficult to fulfill. When tourists from developed countries visit wilderness areas they usually demand high standards of hygiene, good food, clean water, and effective waste disposal, all of which are difficult to achieve in remote areas. The natural wilderness found in the tundra regions of the world, both polar and alpine, provides an ideal target for the development of ecotourism. But providing for the needs of the ecotourists, especially waste disposal, places a strain on the resources of the regions they have come to enjoy.

for the tourists and remove all the waste generated by the same means. Waste disposal is a particularly important consideration in such cold climates where natural decomposition is slow, and tourists who wish to visit such sites can disturb the natural ecosystems by depositing waste materials. The ecotourist is also in danger of disturbing the wildlife by approaching animals too closely, or by trampling sensitive plants. In the Antarctic, for example, visits to seal and penguin colonies are very popular, and the animals often show little fear of humans. But this can encourage very close approaches, which cause stress to seals and penguins with young. There is also the constant danger that visitors will inadvertently bring diseases that will endanger wildlife populations. Heavy trampling on fragile tundra soils and the possibility of contamination from spills of fuel and toxins add to the dangers inherent in wilderness tourism. Conservation authorities often impose strict controls on both the number and the activities of visiting parties in the Arctic and the Antarctic.

Alpine habitats have an even longer history of eco-tourism. Mountaineering, climbing, and hiking became popular activities in the 19th century among those rich enough to afford the travel, the equipment, and the local guides. People who visited mountains were often naturalists who were eager to collect both the plants and animals they discovered, thus destroying some of the wildlife that had attracted them to these locations. Others were "sportsmen" whose main concern was to kill and collect larger specimens of mammals and birds as trophies. As in the case of polar ecotourism, the modern emphasis of alpine ecotourism is upon observation rather than destruction. Despite this, the greater accessibility of the mountains to a larger proportion of the population places new kinds of stress upon alpine tundra habitats. Excessive trampling erodes trails. Waste disposal becomes a particular problem because it is not always possible for visitors to take all of their waste products away with them. In areas of the Himalaya Mountains in Asia, for example, regions of picturesque mountain landscape have become scarred by deposits of litter and other waste materials along the well-used trails. Ecotourism in the mountains therefore requires careful planning and investment. Tourist sites must provide properly equipped camping areas, including latrines and waste-disposal systems, or they will become littered and spoiled. But local people may find great difficulty in providing such facilities in remote and poor countries like Nepal.

The economics of ecotourism form an important consideration. If the wild and beautiful places of the world are to be conserved there must be some financial incentive for the people who live there. In areas like the Himalayas, for example, the arrival of visitors can result in economic gain for the local people, but if this leads to the development of sophisticated hotels to house the visitors, then the money may flow into the pockets of developers from outside the region. Even food may be imported because local produce may not be to the tastes of foreign visitors. There is also the danger that local communities will be disrupted and cultures changed by the presence of tourists. In many instances, local cultures effectively become converted into museum displays, or even circus shows, for the sake of visitor entertainment. The dangers of ecotourism are therefore considerable.

Ecotourism is one way in which tundra habitats are providing leisure activities for people; sport is another. Mountain tundra has also become an important location for winter sports, especially skiing, and this has led to new threats to this wilderness habitat. The skiing industry now attracts large numbers of people to locations that were once deserted or occupied only by small farms and villages. This new influx of people has led to extensive development of roads and residential complexes. Even more serious for the tundra habitat has been the construction of ski runs and ski lifts that greatly modify the landscape. Most of the activity, of course, takes place in winter when the tundra is covered with snow, but the major damage occurs early and late in the season when the snow cover is thin and bare areas of grass are visible. These brown patches on ski runs are the sites of major damage to the underlying vegetation and soil, as pressure, friction, and physical wear degrade them. In summer, the ski run is usually easy to recognize because of its poorer vegetation cover and much lower plant diversity, caused by this damage from the skis. Recreation is important for people and it is inevitable that the mountain landscape should attract winter sports. As in the case of ecotourism, however, excessive use can damage the very resource that provides the pleasure, and users must bear this in mind. Additionally, reserves for wildlife conservation need to be established to ensure that disturbance and damage do not extend into all available habitats.

The value of all tundra habitats, like that of other wilderness areas, is real but it is difficult to translate into economic terms. Wildness has a great appeal to the human spirit, which is why artists, writers, and poets have long extolled the beauty and the appeal of remote locations free from the impact of human society. Most people are inspired by pictures or descriptions of wild places and many will go to great lengths in order to visit such locations and experience silence and solitude at first hand. But even people who may never have the opportunity to visit the wilderness may gain pleasure from the simple knowledge that it exists and that there are still relatively uncontaminated places on the Earth. Polar and alpine tundra, therefore, are of great value to all humanity as a source of inspiration and inner peace.

## Tundra as a carbon sink

Another way in which the tundra serves humanity and, indeed, the general health of the planet, is by acting as a "sink" for atmospheric carbon. The value of tundra in this manner may not be immediately apparent, but is nonetheless important.

Scientists have been monitoring the level of the gas carbon dioxide in the atmosphere for many years. They have also been able to extract trapped bubbles of atmospheric gas from ice sheets and have analyzed the bubbles to produce a record of atmospheric composition in the more distant past. These studies have shown that carbon dioxide has been rising steadily for about 200 years. This period corresponds to that of human industrial development powered by fossil fuels, which contain carbon. People have been burning ancient reserves of carbon in the form of coal, oil, and gas, buried in the rocks, to generate the energy used for daily living. The increase in atmospheric carbon dioxide over those 200 years may not seem very great, from around 0.028 percent to 0.038 percent by volume of the atmosphere. This is a very small concentration of this gas, and a relatively small increase, but most atmospheric scientists believe that its impact on the climate has been considerable. Global temperature has risen by about 3°F (1.5°C) during the same 200 years, and it seems likely that the rise in carbon dioxide has been an important contributing factor to this increase. Carbon dioxide, together with several other gases, acts as a kind of thermal blanket around the Earth, allowing the Sun's rays to penetrate and warm the Earth's surface but preventing the heat generated from escaping back into space. This is the same principle that operates in a greenhouse, hence the expression "greenhouse effect" for this process.

If atmospheric carbon dioxide concentrations continue to rise, then additional increases in global temperature and considerable changes in the Earth's climatic patterns are likely, most of which would be harmful for human populations and for wildlife conservation. Any ecosystem that takes up more carbon dioxide from the atmosphere by photosynthesis or by any other chemical process than it releases to the atmosphere by respiration (called a "carbon sink") must be regarded as valuable and worthy of protection. Growing forests are carbon sinks, as are wetlands. The forest is storing up carbon as new tree biomass, while the wetland creates organic mud and peat in which carbon is stored. The tundra biome, especially the tundra habitats of the Arctic, is also currently a sink for carbon. As discussed in chapter 3, decomposition in tundra is slow and organic materials can accumulate in soils (see "Tundra food webs and energy flow," pages 72–76). In wetter sites, which are frequent in the tundra regions of the Arctic, peat develops and forms a store of carbon. The tundra, therefore, is acting as a sink for atmospheric carbon and will continue to do so while its conditions remain cold and damp. One of the major concerns about the future of the tundra is whether this will continue to be the case.

## Conclusions

Despite the fact that tundra habitats are generally remote and difficult to access, people have used them for a variety of purposes. Tundra has been and continues to be a source of economic profit in many respects, but it also has certain values that are not immediately evident.

Tundra supports many large mammals, including caribou, arctic fox, seals, and polar bears, and the meat and skins of these animals have formed the basis of certain human cultures since the Ice Age. In more recent times, hunters and trappers have continued to exploit this resource, which has been the basis of economically important trade. In most cases, the hunting and trapping of animals in the tundra has concentrated on truly wild animals, but in the case of the European and Asian herds of caribou, or reindeer, a degree of domestication has taken place. Reindeer herding by the Sami people is the only type of agriculture practiced in the tundra.

The rocks of the tundra contain many minerals that have attracted human attention. Metals such as gold have generated mass human migrations in search of this precious material, and others, such as copper, have led to massive destruction of mountain habitats. In recent times, prospectors have discovered oil and gas reserves in the Arctic. Extractive industries have developed some of these reserves, giving rise to a new series of environmental problems.

The wild quality of the tundra has become a focus for a rapidly expanding tourist industry, both in the polar and the alpine tundra regions of the world. The remote wildness of this habitat is an important source of human inspiration, but it is also fragile and the ecotourism industry needs to be carefully controlled if damage to the source of such recreational and educational enjoyment is to be avoided.

The tundra is one of the few habitats that absorbs more carbon out of the atmosphere than it releases, and this makes the tundra biome particularly valuable. This is a hidden use of the tundra that must be appreciated.

The tundra biome thus has many uses and is valuable to humans for a wide range of reasons. Although one of the most remote and inaccessible of the Earth's biomes, it is still in danger of damage and destruction by human activities, so its future lies in human hands.

# CHAPTER 7

# THE FUTURE
# OF THE TUNDRA

The tundra is home to many highly adapted plants and animals, which have developed the attributes needed to survive in an extreme environment. But despite the hardy nature of many of its inhabitants, the tundra is a fragile ecosystem. It is low in biodiversity, so it is in danger of collapsing if any of its component species become extinct. Its nutrient capital and its productivity are low, so the ecosystem may be sensitive to disruption, whether by changing climate or human disturbance. Its soils are unstable, easily damaged and easily eroded. The tundra, therefore, is a biome that is in danger, and the problems that face it need to be considered carefully.

## Consequences of climate change

The Earth is becoming warmer. As discussed in chapter 6, this is probably due in part to human activity, which is increasing the amounts of carbon dioxide and other greenhouse gases in the atmosphere (see "Tundra as a carbon sink," pages 172–173). But the Earth's climate has experienced many shifts in the past, some of them quite rapid, so the present change in climate may also have a natural component that represents a continuation of the cyclic changes that have long been taking place. Whatever the causes of climate change, its consequences could be very considerable for the Earth's biomes and especially for the tundra biome.

It is impossible to predict with accuracy the climate of the future, but if the present warming trend continues, then the global mean temperature is likely to become between 2°F and 4°F (1°C to 2°C) warmer in 2050 than it is at present. This may not seem very much, but it could have considerable geographical and biological consequences, and these consequences will not be evenly spread over the face of the Earth because the warming process will not be the same in all locations. Observations of the increased temperature over the past 50 years show that the high latitudes, which include the regions of polar tundra, have become warmer much faster than the equatorial latitudes. If this trend continues into the future, then the polar latitudes may undergo a greater change in climate than anywhere else on Earth.

The tundra biome contains the world's reserves of ice, and a warmer climate will mean that some, perhaps most, of this reserve will melt and join the oceans. It is quite possible that the Greenland ice sheet will have melted by the end of the 21st century, and this would add considerably to the level of the world's oceans. The floating pack ice of the Arctic Ocean is melting and, if the process continues at the present rate, may disappear completely by about 2070. The Antarctic ice sheet is more difficult to predict. Current evidence shows that the surrounding sea ice is breaking up extensively, but in the long term much will depend on levels of precipitation. Warmer sea temperature means faster evaporation of water, and this could bring more precipitation over Antarctica. More snow would fall over the vast ice sheet, so the ice volume might not decline as fast as expected on the basis of future temperature calculations. So there are still some important unknown factors in the equation. Water expands when it is heated, so increasing the temperature of the world's oceans will cause an expansion that will raise sea levels globally. Taking into account the combined effects of melting ice and expanding water, observers widely expect the level of the Earth's oceans to rise by four to 10 inches (10–25 cm) by 2050. A sea level rise of this magnitude would flood many coastal areas of Arctic tundra. But, on the other hand, the loss of ice and snow over the tundra landscape will expose more elevated land areas where tundra vegetation can invade.

While the rising sea level erodes the polar tundra from the Arctic Ocean in the north, vegetation changes will also take place from the south. At the boundary between the tundra and the boreal forest (or taiga) in the Low Arctic, warmer conditions will enable trees to bear fruit and spread their seeds into new regions. The forest will advance northward into regions that are now covered by low shrubs and cushion herbs. There is already evidence of spruce invading beyond its former limits in Canada and extending the boreal forest into the tundra zone. The tundra biome, therefore, will become squeezed between the forest and the sea, and it is likely to occupy an increasingly narrow zone as climate warms.

Meanwhile, in the mountains of the world the warmer temperatures will cause the tree line to extend upward and the line of permanent snow will retreat. This means that the belt of tundra will gradually occupy higher altitudes. But this process can continue only until the permanent snow zone is completely lost, and snow loss will depend upon the latitudinal position of the mountain (equatorial mountains will lose their snow first) and the overall altitude of the mountain (higher mountains will retain their snow longer). In the case of low mountains in warm, low-latitude climates, increased warmth will eventually eliminate alpine tundra vegetation. As the trees spread upward the tundra plants will have nowhere to retreat to and will eventually become shaded out by the expanding forest. Studies of mountains in the high latitudes, especially those in the polar regions, suggest that high winds may prevent forest expansion even though the air temperature may rise. These mountains, particularly those of the Arctic, may become the final refuge for tundra in a warmer world.

The prospects for the tundra biome in the event of continued climatic warming may therefore appear rather bleak. But the tundra has survived as a biome for several million years, despite episodes in the Earth's recent past that were much warmer than the present world. This suggests that the tundra has a higher degree of inertia, or resistance to change, than one might expect. Two possible reasons have been put forward to explain this. First, the very low levels of nutrients in tundra soils may actually help in the survival of this biome. Chapter 4 proposed that low nutrient reserves might make an ecosystem fragile; but poor soils could also make the tundra difficult to invade. Trees generally need more chemical nutrients than smaller plants do, and most trees find it difficult to establish themselves in poor soils. Even the tough birches, pines, and spruces that occupy the border regions of the Arctic tundra find it difficult to germinate and survive in very poor soils, especially when they are being grazed upon by voracious herbivores such as arctic hares and caribou. So, nutrient poverty may actually protect the tundra from tree invasion.

The second feature that the tundra biome has in its favor is a high level of genetic diversity in its flora and fauna. Earlier discussion has stressed that the number of species of plants and animals in the tundra is low, but among the species present there are many subspecies and races. The environment itself is quite diverse, with wet locations and dry ones, salty and fresh areas, high altitudes and low, exposed and protected areas, snow-covered and open locations. The species of plants and animals present, though low in number, have developed a whole range of genetically adapted forms, called *ecotypes,* that are able to cope in each of these different microhabitats. This genetic diversity will greatly assist the tundra as it faces the challenge of climate change. Whatever new sets of conditions are generated by the changes, it is likely that many existing species will have the right set of genetic adaptations to take advantage of the new opportunities. Perhaps this high genetic diversity is what has enabled the tundra to survive the many occasions when climate change has threatened this biome in the past.

## Ozone holes

Apart from climate change, another aspect of changing global conditions that has attracted attention in recent years is the development of gaps in the ozone layer, especially in polar regions. These may present a further threat to the health of the tundra biome.

It is easy to become confused about the gas ozone. It is a very reactive material, having the chemical formula $O_3$ and possessing great powers of oxidation. It attacks many types of materials and can even decompose rubber. When people breathe it in, therefore, it damages the lungs and can prove fatal to those with weak respiratory systems. Produced from the chemical reactions of oxides of nitrogen, ozone is one component of automobile exhaust fumes, and when coupled with strong sunlight and other products of combustion it can contribute to the formation of photochemical smog. So, ozone close to the Earth's surface, especially in sunny cities, is a pollutant gas that is a health risk and needs to be avoided.

But ozone also occurs naturally, high in the stratosphere, which is a layer of the Earth's atmosphere lying about six to 30 miles (10 to 50 km) above the ground. Even in the stratosphere, ozone is only a trace gas, and if all the ozone present in the stratosphere were concentrated at ground level under normal atmospheric pressure, it would form a layer only 0.1 inch (3 mm) thick. But this small amount of ozone in the stratosphere performs a vital function for all the living things on the land surface of the Earth; it absorbs the harmful ultraviolet (UV) radiation from the Sun. In the absence of such protection the UV radiation would cause genetic damage among all living things, apart from those living deep in the oceans, where they are protected by the ozone-screening effect of water.

Research into the changes in atmospheric ozone began in 1957 when atmospheric scientists set up an international network of monitoring stations, including one in Antarctica. By 1985 sufficient data had been accumulated to demonstrate that the overall quantity of ozone in the stratosphere, particularly over the Antarctic, had severely declined during the period of monitoring. Its concentration had halved since 1957. Detailed studies showed that the loss of ozone was seasonal, with the strongest decline occurring in the Antarctic spring. Two possible causes were investigated: first, the increasing abundance of stratospheric jet traffic, and second, the release by humans of increasing quantities of a group of chemicals called chlorofluorocarbons (CFCs), used in aerosol sprays, refrigerators, and the production of plastic foam. Little evidence could be found to support the jet plane hypothesis, but CFC release became an increasingly likely explanation for the development of an "ozone hole" over the Antarctic. CFCs are released at the Earth's surface and then diffuse upward through the atmosphere, gradually breaking down to release chlorine, which then interacts with ozone, causing its decomposition to oxygen. Due to circulation patterns in the atmosphere ozone destruction is greatest in the South Pole region, but an ozone hole has also been developing above the Arctic in recent years. In September 2000 the ozone hole over the Antarctic extended over a record 11 million square miles (29 million km$^2$). This is an area three times that of the United States and it covered the whole of Antarctica, together with much of the Southern Ocean and even the southern tip of Chile. The threat to the health of people and wildlife is so severe that many nations have agreed upon a policy to reduce the rate of ozone destruction, which has been set out in the Montreal Protocol (see sidebar below). By 2005 there are some small signs of ozone recovery.

## Pollution

Pollution by human waste products and accidental spills threatens all of the Earth's ecosystems, but particularly the sensitive tundra biome. As discussed in chapter 6, the exploitation of the mineral resources of the tundra regions has often been accompanied by pollution and consequent environmental damage (see "Mineral reserves," pages 163–168). Oil spills at the site of extraction, or during transport by pipeline or

### *The Vienna Convention and the Montreal Protocol*

In 1985, 20 nations agreed that they needed to act swiftly to protect human health and control the expansion of the polar ozone holes. They signed the Vienna Convention, which was a statement of intent to take action, though it did not state precisely what action was needed. In 1987 a further international meeting in Canada led to the Montreal Protocol, an agreement to restrict the production and use of compounds such as CFCs that are known to affect the ozone layer. Those signing the protocol have put its provisions into effect, especially the developed nations, which are responsible for the bulk of CFC production. In total, 155 nations have now agreed to the proposals of the Montreal Protocol, of which more than 100 are developed nations. The outcome has been a slowing in the rate of ozone destruction, so that the polar tundra, and the humans who live and work in the tundra, appear to have been rescued from a most unpleasant fate.

ship, are statistically inevitable, given the large quantities taken out of the rocks beneath the tundra and the long distances the materials have to be moved for their treatment and consumption. Contamination of rivers and soils from mining waste is likewise an unavoidable outcome during the extraction of metals from the rocks beneath the tundra. Waste products from human settlements are difficult to dispose of, and they create pollution and health problems. All of these sources of pollution are local to the tundra, and the best way to prevent them is to control the extent of exploitation of the habitat, possibly even denying humans the right to commence such exploitation, as in the case of mineral extraction in Antarctica. But there are other sources of pollution that are distant from the tundra regions and more difficult to control.

Pesticides are extensively used throughout the world as a means of increasing the yield of crops or the health and productivity of domesticated animals. They are toxins that are selected to kill some organisms (such as insect pests) without causing harm to others, including people. But scientists and agriculturalists have often miscalculated and used pesticides that had a harmful impact beyond the target organism. The use of DDT to kill insects in the 1940s and 1950s, for example, was very successful in the control of many insect-borne diseases, including malaria, so it undoubtedly saved many thousands of human lives, including those of soldiers during World War II. But the compound proved very durable in the environment. Its concentration built up in the fat reserves of birds and mammals until it eventually impaired their breeding and sometimes even caused their death. DDT also spread around the world, finding its way through marine food webs to the tundra regions and accumulating in the fatty tissues of seals and penguins. Fortunately, the harmful effects of this compound were recognized in time, and most developed countries have now banned the use of DDT. The persistence of this chemical in the environment is limited; within 10 years half of any residual DDT will decompose, so the threat of global contamination is now reduced. The withdrawal of this compound in many parts of the world should prevent the destruction of tundra mammals and birds, as well as those of other biomes.

Most pesticides, including DDT, are artificial compounds, so their origin as pollutants is never in doubt, even when they are found in remote areas such as the Antarctic. But people produce other materials that also occur naturally, so it is less easy to be sure of their source. Nitrogen compounds, including ammonia and oxides of nitrogen, for example, occur naturally in the atmosphere, but exhaust gases from traffic, together with fertilizers that farmers spray, have injected more of these materials into the atmosphere. They are pollutants, but because nitrogen is an important element for the growth and development of plants they are also growth stimulants for vegetation (see "Nutrient cycling in the tundra," pages 76–81). Tundra soils are poor in nitrogen, so the arrival of the element from the air can change the vegetation composition; more robust and fast-growing plants outcompete the slower and weaker species. This can lead to the extinction of the less competitive species.

Scientists studying the aerial fallout of nitrogen compounds in the Arctic have found that the quantities arriving are minute, usually between 0.0027 and 0.027 ounces per square yard (0.1 to 1.0 $g/m^2$) in a year. This may seem very small, but in fact it is as great as the combined total of all other sources of nitrogen in the ecosystem, such as the breakdown of soil materials by decomposition and weathering and the fixation of atmospheric nitrogen by bacteria. Air pollution, in other words, has roughly doubled the nitrogen supply to the tundra ecosystem. In the future, this change in nutrient cycling is likely to encourage more robust vegetation growth, permitting more shrubs and trees to invade the open tundra. This fertilization of the soils by pollutants, combined with the likely effects of climate warming, raises a strong possibility that the forest will spread into the tundra. Here lies the greatest threat to the future of the tundra biome.

## Tundra conservation

For the tundra to remain as one of the Earth's major biomes, people must conserve it. Conservation is not quite the same thing as preservation. In preservation, one isolates an object from injurious influences and protects it to ensure that it remains unaltered by events. In the natural world this would be an impossible task because the natural environment itself is constantly changing. Climate changes partly because of natural cycles, and unpredictable events such as wind, earthquake, fire, and flood can disrupt natural ecosystems. Humans, as has been seen, extend their influence far beyond the regions they inhabit, so even the most remote of wildernesses cannot be fully protected from the effects of human activity. Conservation, therefore, aims to protect but also to manage the ecosystem in order to modify or control the pressures that come from outside. There was a time when ecologists believed that the best form of conservation was to leave an ecosystem alone and to avoid any form of human intervention. It is now recognized that this attitude is based on an impossible ideal and that people need to actively manage ecosystems in order to maintain levels of biodiversity on Earth.

In the polar tundra, protection from the harmful human impacts is clearly the first priority. The hunting of mammals needs to be controlled if their populations are to remain stable. In the case of some animals, such as the great whales, controlling hunting may mean stopping it entirely, but with others, such as seals and caribou, there may be a case for limited harvesting of the herds. Indeed, there are occasions when culling of populations is a humane reaction to overpopulation. For instance, the red deer (elk) population on the alpine tundra habitats of Scotland has recently expanded, with numbers increasing fourfold between 1960 and 2000. The alpine tundra habitat is becoming damaged, and each winter a proportion of the elk inevitably starve. The imbalance was the result of past human activity, namely eliminating the wolf from Scotland (the last wolf was shot in 1743). Now this large deer has no natural predators. There is, however, a new herbivore in the alpine tundra that people have introduced, namely the sheep, and herds of sheep contribute to overgrazing and vegetation destruction. In response, human management of the Scottish Highland tundra must reduce either sheep grazing or deer numbers, or both. Already, hunters take about 50,000 red deer every year in

Scotland, representing approximately 13 percent of the population. Clearly, however, this is not enough to stabilize the population, and further culling may prove necessary.

The control of Scottish red deer is an example of the need to manage ecosystems, especially if they have already been modified by human activity and left unbalanced. Sometimes it is necessary to try to put right errors of the past, such as the local extinction of a species. Reintroduction of the lost animal is always controversial for many reasons. It may bring problems for human populations. If the wolf were to be reintroduced to Scotland, for instance, sheep farmers would undoubtedly object, just as farmers have done near Yellowstone National Park, where wolves have been successfully reintroduced (see sidebar on opposite page). The musk ox is a species that has attracted less controversy than the wolf but has suffered even more at the hands of human hunters. Once widespread through the Arctic, it became very restricted as a result of a long history of hunting from prehistoric to modern times. It was completely lost from Europe, Asia, and Alaska, but the surviving herds on Greenland have formed the basis for reintroduction to Russia and to Alaska. In some sites the introduced musk oxen have found it difficult to compete with native caribou herds, but generally the species seems to be holding its own. In the case of the musk ox, where humans have been responsible for local extinctions, it seems only reasonable that humans should try to set things straight by reintroduction. One of the dangers of this strategy, however, is that the stock may be taken from herds with slightly different genetic makeup. In the process of reintroduction, the conservationist may be taking animals and plants to regions where they are not fully suited for survival.

In alpine tundra habitats, local extinction is a very common problem because of the isolation of mountain peaks. If an animal or plant is lost at one site, it may be difficult for the species to reinvade from surrounding but isolated mountains. Reintroduction of animals lost as a result of human persecution has therefore been extensively used in mountain regions. In North America, the mountain goat has been reestablished in Oregon, Nevada, Utah, Colorado, Wyoming, and South Dakota from its residual populations in the north-

## Bringing back the wolf

Throughout the world, people generally regard wolves as pests. Livestock farmers, in particular, are invariably eager to eliminate this intelligent, pack-hunting predator. In the United States (with the exception of Alaska) the gray wolf had been reduced to a few small populations in the northern parts of the country by the middle of the 20th century; even in Yellowstone National Park, the last wolf was shot in 1926. But after 70 years without wolves, conservationists became concerned that the whole ecological balance of Yellowstone had been altered because of the loss of wolves. One of the main prey species in the park had been elk, and in the absence of the top predator, elk populations expanded and forests were overgrazed. Wolves, it seemed, had an indirect impact on the balance of forest trees. In 1995 the U.S. Fish and Wildlife Service introduced 15 gray wolves from Canada into Yellowstone, and they proved so successful that they now number around 300. Elk populations have reduced and new habitats have been created, especially around lakes where elk grazing was particularly intense. The remains of dead elk, killed by wolves, provide food for bears, ravens, and eagles. In short, the return of the wolf has increased the biodiversity of the park.

ern Rocky Mountains and Cascades. The closely related chamois of the European Alps was similarly severely reduced by hunting but has recovered much of its former range as a result of reintroduction.

Conservationists have also helped some birds to spread back into mountain areas where they had previously been exterminated. The bearded vulture of Europe and Asia is a massive bird that feeds on broken bones that it drops onto rocks from the air, and it has benefited from human transport and care in bringing it back to several mountain ranges from which it had been lost as a result of human persecution.

Human beings are now so numerous and so influential in polluting the atmosphere and the oceans that there is no part of the planet left unaffected. Even the remote areas of tundra, both polar and alpine, have experienced change as a result of the arrival of humans on the scene. As discussed in chapter 6, the tundra is a useful biome for people because of its mineral wealth, its recreational opportunities, and its role in the overall balance of the planet. People, therefore, will need to play

an increasing part in the conservation of tundra, both pro-
tecting it from further harm and putting right some of the
problems this biome has already suffered as a consequence of
human errors. The future of the tundra, as is the case for all
biomes, now lies in human hands.

## Conclusions

The tundra biome, both in the polar regions and in the
mountains of the world, faces a number of problems, some of
which threaten its very survival. Continued climatic warming is almost certain, and this will have a particular impact
on the Earth's coldest biome. Tundra lies at the world's
extremities, either close to the poles or near the highest parts
of mountains. There is no place to which tundra can retreat if
warming continues; it may be eliminated from the tops of
mountains (windy Arctic mountains are a possible exception)
and become confined to an increasingly narrow belt of land
south of the Arctic Ocean. The likely rise in global sea level in
the warmer world can only make things worse. Added to this,
it seems probable that the polar regions will experience more
rapid rises in temperature over the next century than most
other places on Earth. Many of the highly adapted cold-tolerant species of plants and animals will find themselves under
climatic and spatial stress, eliminated by stronger, more competitive, warmth-loving species. The one hope for tundra biodiversity is its great genetic variability. The organisms of the
tundra are not only highly adapted but also highly adaptable, and this may prove vital for their survival.

Ozone depletion in the polar stratosphere has posed a new
threat to the tundra because it permits higher levels of ultraviolet radiation from the Sun to penetrate the atmosphere.
This can cause genetic damage to exposed tissues. The
human causes of ozone thinning appear to have been identified, and the efforts of many nations to reduce this potentially serious threat to tundra survival may prove successful.

Pollution, both in the form of direct deposition of harmful
compounds and in the less obvious form of atmospheric and
oceanic contamination, is a further source of damage to the
tundra. People must make pollution control a priority to protect this biome.

Conservation of the tundra, therefore, will involve the enforcement of protective measures at an international level, and many of these are already agreed upon and in place. But conservation demands more than just protection; it requires proactive management. Human activities have reduced the ranges of certain species, and these organisms may require human assistance to reestablish themselves over their former ranges. Meanwhile, some species may need to be controlled to avoid excessive use of resources, and some habitats may need to be modified to ensure the survival of sensitive species. The tundra is useful to humans, as well as being valuable in its own right, and the future of the tundra lies very much in human hands.

# GLOSSARY

**ablation**   the loss of ice at the base of a glacier, where the warmth of the Earth causes melting

**active layer**   the upper soil layers in Arctic permafrost environments that melt in the summer and freeze in the winter

**aestivation**   a period of dormancy that certain animals undergo to avoid the unfavorable conditions of summer drought (equivalent to hibernation in winter)

**albedo**   an index of the degree of reflectivity of a surface to light. Snow has a high albedo; dark-colored vegetation has a low albedo

**allochthonous**   describing material that has originated away from the site in which it eventually settles, such as leaves carried into a lake; the opposite of autochthonous

**allogenic**   describing forces outside a particular ecosystem that may cause internal changes; for instance, rising sea level can influence water tables in freshwater wetlands farther inland, and is therefore considered an allogenic factor

**alpine tundra**   vegetation dominated by herbs and dwarf shrubs found above the tree line of high mountains, where conditions are too cold for tree growth

**anaerobic**   lacking oxygen

**anion**   elements or groups of elements carrying a negative charge, such as $NO_3^-$ or $HPO_3^-$

**annual**   an organism (usually a plant) that completes its life cycle in a single year

**anoxic**   lacking oxygen

**Arctic-alpine**   describing an organism that is found in both Arctic and alpine tundra habitats

**Arctic tundra**   a region with vegetation dominated by herbs and dwarf shrubs found in the polar regions where conditions are too cold for tree growth

**aspect**   the direction of the compass that a slope faces

**autochthonous**   describing material that has originated in the site where it is deposited, such as bog moss peat in a bog; the opposite of allochthonous

**autogenic**   describing forces within an ecosystem that bring about changes. For instance, the growth of reeds in a marsh results in increased sediment deposition. *See also* FACILITATION

**biodiversity**   the full range of living things found in an area, together with the variety of genetic constitutions within those species and the range of habitats available at the site

**biogeography**   the scientific study of the spatial distribution of living animals and plants

**biomass**   the quantity of living material within an ecosystem, including those parts of living organisms that are part of them but are strictly nonliving (such as wood, hair, teeth, or claws) but excluding separate dead materials on the ground or in the soil (termed *litter*)

**biosphere**   those parts of the Earth and its atmosphere in which living things are able to exist

**blue-green bacteria (cyanobacteria)**   microscopic, colonial, photosynthetic microbes that are able to fix nitrogen; once wrongly called blue-green algae. They play important ecological roles in some wetlands as a consequence of their nitrogen-fixing ability, such as in rice paddies

**bog**   a wetland ecosystem in which the water supply is entirely from rainfall (ombrotrophic). Such wetlands are acidic and poor in nutrient elements. They accumulate a purely organic peat with very little mineral matter (derived solely from airborne dust), so are prized for horticulture

**boreal**   northern, usually referring to the northern temperate regions of North America and Eurasia, which are typically vegetated by evergreen coniferous forests and wetlands. Named after Boreas, the Greek god of the North Wind

**calcareous**   rich in calcium carbonate (lime)

**capillaries**   fine, tubelike air spaces found in the structure of partially compacted peat or soils

**carbon sink**   an ecosystem that absorbs more carbon from the atmosphere than it releases in respiration. Some wetland habitats operate in this way

**catchment**   a region drained by a stream or river system (equivalent to watershed)

**cation**   an element or group of elements with a positive charge, such as $Na^+$, $NH_4^+$, or $Ca^{++}$

**cation exchange**   the substitution of one positively charged ion for another. Certain materials (such as peat and clay) have the capacity to attract and retain cations and to exchange them for hydrogen in the process of leaching

**chamaephyte** a plant that grows close to the surface of the ground, below a height of one foot (25 cm), and in this way escapes the effects of intense wind-blasting in tundra habitats

**charcoal** incompletely burned pieces of organic material (usually plant). These are virtually inert and hence become incorporated into lake sediments and peat deposits, where they provide useful indications of former fires. Fine charcoal particles may cause changes in the drainage properties of soils, blocking soil capillaries and leading to waterlogging

**climate** the average set of weather conditions over a long period in a region

**climax** the supposed final, equilibrium stage of an ecological succession. Many would question whether real stability in nature is ever achieved

**community** an assemblage of different plant and animal species, all found living and interacting together. Although they may give the appearance of stability, communities are constantly changing as species respond in different ways to such environmental alterations as climate change

**competition** an interaction between two individuals of the same or different species arising from the need of both for a particular resource that is in short supply. Competition usually results in harm to one or both competitors

**conservation** human protection and enhancement of a habitat or a species

**cyanobacteria** *see* BLUE-GREEN BACTERIA

**day length** the period from sunrise to sunset. This may be nonexistent in a polar winter

**deciduous** describing a plant that loses all its leaves during an unfavorable season, which may be particularly cold or particularly dry

**decomposition** the process by which organic matter is reduced in complexity as microbes use its energy content, usually by a process of oxidation. As living things respire the organic materials producing carbon dioxide, other elements such as phosphorus and nitrogen return to the environment where they are available to living organisms once more. Decomposition is therefore an important aspect of the nutrient cycle

**detritivore** an animal (usually invertebrate) that feeds upon dead organic matter

**diatoms** a group of one-celled photosynthetic organisms that form an important part of the phytoplankton in wetland habitats

**DNA**   deoxyribonucleic acid, the molecule that contains the genetic code

**drumlin**   a deposit of till beneath a glacier that is often carved into a linear shape by the movement of the ice above

**ecosystem**   an ecological unit of study encompassing the living organisms together with the nonliving environment within a particular habitat

**ecotone**   boundary regions where one type of habitat gradually blends into another

**ecotourism**   tourism to wilderness areas of the world that tries to avoid damaging the environment in its development

**emergent aquatic plants**   wetland plants that are rooted in soil that lies underneath but have shoots projecting above the water surface

**energy flow**   the movement of energy through an ecosystem, from sunlight energy fixation in photosynthesis to its acquisition by consumer organisms and its release by respiration

**erosion**   the degradation and removal of materials from one location to another, often by means of water or wind

**erratic**   a rock that is carried far from its original position by the movement of a glacier and is eventually deposited when the glacier melts

**esker**   a ridge of glacial detritus running along the edge of a glacier or beneath the ice

**eutrophication**   an increase of fertility within a habitat, often resulting from pollution by nitrates or phosphate from runoff of these materials into water bodies from surrounding land. Although the term most often describes wetland habitats, it can also be applied to terrestrial ecosystems, such as the tundra

**evaporation**   the conversion of a liquid to its gaseous phase, especially the loss of water from terrestrial and aquatic surfaces

**evapotranspiration**   a combination of evaporation from land and water surfaces and the loss of water vapor from plant leaves (transpiration)

**evergreen**   a leaf or a plant that remains green and potentially able to photosynthesize throughout the year. Evergreen leaves do eventually fall, but may last for several seasons before they do so

**facilitation**   the process by which a plant species alters its local environment such that other plants can invade. For example, when a water lily grows in a lake, its leaf stalks slow the movement of water, causing suspended sediments to settle. The lake consequently becomes shallower, permitting other plant species to invade and eventually supplant the water lily. Facilitation is one of the forces that drives ecological succession

**firn** powdery or granular deposits of snow that accumulate on the surface of a glacier

**fjord** a deep, steep-sided valley flooded by the sea

**floodplain** the low-lying lands alongside a river over which the river water expands when water flows faster than the river can carry it away

**fluvial outwash** the detritus washed out of a glacier as it melts

**food web** the complex interaction of animal feeding patterns in an ecosystem

**forest tundra** the ecotone (border region) of the forest and the tundra. Trees that survive here are usually dwarfs, stunted by strong winds, and are referred to as KRUMMHOLZ

**fossil** ancient remains, usually the buried remnants of a once-living organism; the term can also be applied to ancient buried soils or even the organic remains termed fossil fuels

**fragility** an expression of the ease with which an organism or a habitat may be damaged. Fragile ecosystems, such as many wetlands, need careful conservation

**frost heaving** the mechanism of freezing and thawing of a soil that forces stones and unfrozen layers of soil to the surface

**fundamental niche** the potential of an organism to perform certain functions or to live in certain areas. Such potential is not always achieved because of competitive interactions with other organisms. *See also* REALIZED NICHE

**genes** the store of hereditary information of living things, which is made up of DNA and contained within an organism's cells

**glacier** a mass of permanent ice found in cold conditions, often occupying valleys through which the ice moves slowly under the influence of gravity

**glacial** a period in the Earth's history when conditions are cold enough for glaciers to be widespread

**gley** a pale gray soil produced by permanent waterlogging

**greenhouse effect** the warming of the Earth's surface due to the interaction between radiation and the Earth's atmosphere. Short-wave solar radiation passes through the atmosphere unchanged, but the Earth's surface radiates it as long-wave radiation (heat). The atmosphere then absorbs the long-wave radiation because of the presence of greenhouse gases

**greenhouse gas**   an atmospheric gas that absorbs long-wave radiation and therefore contributes to the warming of the Earth's surface by the greenhouse effect. Greenhouse gases include carbon dioxide, water vapor, methane, chlorofluoro-carbons (CFCs), ozone, and oxides of nitrogen

**groundwater**   water that soaks through soils and rocks, as opposed to water derived directly from precipitation and present on the surface of the soil

**habitat**   the place where an organism lives

**habitat structure**   the architecture of vegetation in a habitat. The height and branching patterns of plants contribute to the complexity of vegetation architecture, and this complexity creates microhabitats for animal life

**halophyte**   a plant that is adapted to life in saline conditions as a result of its physical form, its physiology, or both

**hibernation**   a period of dormancy that certain animals undergo to avoid cold winter conditions

**High Arctic**   the northern regions of the Arctic, where the growing season for plants is less than two and a half months

**hydrology**   the study of the movement of water in its cycles through ecosystems and around the planet

**ice sheet**   an extensive cover of permanent deep ice. Only two ice sheets currently occupy the Earth, one covering Antarctica and the other based on Greenland

**ice wedge**   water that freezes in a tundra soil and expands, forming a wedge shape that forces its way down into the soil and may split the landscape into a series of polygons

**inertia**   the property of resistance to disturbance in an ecosystem. A stable ecosystem is difficult to disturb

**interception**   a function of plants in which the plant canopy catches rainwater and prevents it from reaching the ground directly

**interglacial**   a prolonged period of Earth's history in which the climate is warm; interglacials are preceded and followed by glacials

**interstadial**   a geologically short period of warmth, preceded and followed by stadials

**invertebrate**   an animal lacking a backbone

**ion**   a charged element or group of elements. *See also* ANION and CATION

**kettle hole**   a hollow in glacial detritus deposits resulting from the melting of a block of ice in that position. It may become filled with water to form a deep, steep-sided lake

**krummholz**   a vegetation dominated by trees that have been distorted and stunted by strong winds. *See also* FOREST TUNDRA

**lapse rate**   the rate at which atmospheric temperature drops with altitude

**latitude**   imaginary lines drawn horizontally around the Earth that are named according to the angle they make with the center of the Earth. Thus, the equator is 0°N and S latitude and the poles are 90°N and 90°S. The polar regions thus have higher numbers and are referred to as high latitudes

**leaching**   the process by which ions are lost from soils and sediments as water (particularly acidic water) passes through them

**lichen**   an organism that consists of a combination of an alga or a cyanobacterium with a fungus. The combination may have a leafy form or may look like paint on a rock. Lichens are generally resistant to cold and drought

**limestone**   sedimentary rocks containing a high proportion of calcium carbonate (lime)

**litter**   the accumulation of dead (mainly plant) organic material on the surface of a soil

**loess**   windblown dust and sand carried by winds over bare, glacial terrain

**Low Arctic**   the southern regions of the Arctic, where the growing season for vegetation is generally between three and five months

**macrophyte**   large aquatic plants that can be observed without the use of a microscope

**management**   the deliberate manipulation of an ecosystem by humans in order to achieve a particular end, such as increased productivity or nature conservation

**megafauna**   extremely large animals, many of which became extinct at the end of the last glacial

**methane**   a gas produced by some living organisms as a result of the incomplete decomposition of organic matter. It is a greenhouse gas, a gas that increases the heat-retention properties of the atmosphere

**methanogenic bacteria**   bacteria that produce methane gas as a result of their metabolism

**microbes**   microscopic organisms such as bacteria, fungi, and viruses

**microclimate**   the small-scale climate within habitats, such as beneath forest canopies or in the shade of rocks. The microclimate is strongly affected by habitat structure

**migration**   the seasonal movements of animal populations, such as geese, caribou, or plankton

**mire**   a general term for any peat-forming wetland ecosystem

**mire complex**   a wetland that consists of a series of different mire types

**moraine**   an unsorted mass of glacial debris deposited at the end of a melting glacier (terminal moraine) or beneath the ice mass (hummocky moraine)

**niche**   the role that a species plays in an ecosystem. The concept of niche consists of both where the species lives and how it makes its living (such as feeding requirements, growth patterns, or reproductive behavior). The niche may be regarded as FUNDAMENTAL or REALIZED

**nidifugous**   describing newly hatched birds that rapidly leave their nest

**nitrogen fixation**   the process by which certain organisms are able to convert nitrogen gas into organic molecules that can be built into proteins

**nunatak**   the peak of a mountain projecting from a mass of ice

**nutrient cycle**   the cyclic pattern of element movements between different parts of the ecosystem, together with the balance of input to and output from the ecosystem

**occult precipitation**   precipitation that is not registered by a standard rain gauge because it arrives as mist, condensing on surfaces, including vegetation canopies. *See* INTERCEPTION

**ombrotrophic**   fed by rainfall. Bogs are ombrotrophic mires, receiving their water and nutrient input solely from atmospheric precipitation

**organism**   any living creature, from bacteria to mammals and plants

**ozone hole**   extreme thinning of the ozone layer over the polar regions in their respective summers, which allows excessive ultraviolet radiation to reach the Earth's surface. Ozone ($O_3$) is an unstable form of oxygen gas ($O_2$)

**paleoecology**   the study of the ecology of past communities using a variety of chemical and biological techniques

**palsa**   a wetland type found only within the Arctic Circle. Elevated peat masses expand as a frozen core develops within them. Palsas pass through a cycle of growth and then collapse, forming open pools. Compare PINGO

**paludification**  a process in which an ecosystem becomes inundated with water

**peat**  organic accumulations in wetlands resulting from the incomplete decomposition of vegetation litter

**periglacial**  describing the climatic conditions found around the edges of a glacier

**permafrost**  permanently frozen subsoil. The upper layer (active layer) thaws during the summer and freezes in winter

**pH**  an index of acidity and alkalinity. Low pH means high concentrations of hydrogen ions (hence acidity), while a high pH indicates strong alkalinity. A pH of seven indicates neutrality. The pH scale is logarithmic, which means, for instance, that pH four is 10 times as acidic as pH five

**photosynthesis**  the process by which certain organisms trap the energy of sunlight using a colored pigment (usually chlorophyll) and use that energy to take carbon dioxide from the atmosphere and convert it into organic molecules, initially sugars

**photosynthetic bacteria**  bacteria possessing pigments enabling them to trap light energy and conduct photosynthesis. Some types are green and others purple

**physiological drought**  a condition in which water is present in a habitat but is unavailable to a plant, for instance because it is frozen

**phytoplankton**  the collection of microscopic, often one-celled photosynthetic organisms that live in the well-lit surface layers of water bodies. They form the basis of many aquatic food webs

**pingo**  a structure formed in the tundra soil by water freezing under pressure, often fed by a spring. As the water turns to ice, it forces the surface of the ground to rise into an extensive mound

**pioneer**  a species that is an initial colonist in a developing habitat

**plate tectonics**  the theory that the crust of the Earth is divided into plates that move over the surface, occasionally colliding and buckling to form mountain chains or deep rifts

**podzol**  a type of soil, common in the boreal forest (or taiga) zone and in the ecotone with the tundra. It consists of a series of layers formed by the leaching of iron, organic matter, and clay from the upper layers and their deposition lower down

**pollen analysis**　the identification and counting of fossil pollen grains and spores stratified in peat deposits and lake sediments

**pollen grains**　cells containing the male genetic information of flowering plants and conifers. The outer coat is robust and survives well in wetland sediments. The distinctive structure and sculpturing of the coats permit their identification even in a fossil form

**polygon mire**　patterned wetlands of the Arctic regions in which raised polygonal sections are separated by water-filled channels, particularly apparent from the air

**polygons**　patterns of stones caused by frost heaving on level ground in tundra habitats

**population**　a collection of individual organisms all of the same species

**precipitation**　aerial deposition of water as rain, dew, snow, or in an occult form

**primary productivity**　the rate at which new organic matter is added to an ecosystem, usually as a result of green plant photosynthesis

**radiocarbon dating**　a technique for establishing the age of a sample of organic matter, based upon the known decay rate of the isotope $^{14}C$ (carbon-14)

**raised bog**　a mire in which peat accumulates to form a central dome that raises the peat-forming vegetation above the influence of groundwater flow. The surface of the central dome thus receives all its water input from precipitation; it is ombrotrophic

**realized niche**　the actual spatial and functional role of a species under competition from other species in an ecosystem. Compare FUNDAMENTAL NICHE

**reclamation**　the conversion of a habitat to a condition appropriate for such human activity as agriculture or forestry

**rehabilitation**　the conversion of a damaged ecosystem back to its original condition

**relict**　a species or a population left behind following the fragmentation and loss of a previously extensive range

**replaceability**　the ease with which a particular habitat can be replaced if it were to be lost

**representativeness**　the degree to which a site illustrates the major features characteristic of its habitat type

**resilience**  the ability of a stable ecosystem to recover rapidly from disturbance

**respiration**  the release of energy from organic food materials by a process of controlled oxidation within the cell. Under aerobic conditions carbon dioxide is released, while anaerobic respiration may lead to the formation of ethyl alcohol

**rheotrophic**  describing a wetland that receives its nutrient elements from both groundwater flow and precipitation. In rheotrophic mires the groundwater flow is usually responsible for the bulk of the nutrient input

**rhizopods**  microscopic organisms resembling *Amoeba,* but with a protective shell around their one-celled bodies. These shells are often preserved as fossils within peat deposits

**salt marsh**  coastal intertidal wetlands dominated by herbaceous plants

**sediment**  material that is deposited in an ecosystem, such as a lake or a peat land, and accumulates over the course of time. Sediments may be organic and/or mineral in their nature

**sedimentation**  the process of sediment accumulation

**snow patch**  an accumulation of snow that is sufficiently deep to survive well into the summer season and may even last for several years. Its edges melt each summer

**solifluction**  the movement of soils down slopes in tundra conditions, which occurs because the surface of the soil melts while the lower layers remain frozen

**spore**  the dispersal structure of algae, mosses, liverworts, ferns, and fungi, from which a new individual can grow

**stadial**  a cold period in the history of the Earth that is less severe or shorter than a glacial episode

**stone stripes**  lines of stones following the contours of a slope that are produced by frost-heaving in tundra soils

**stratification**  the layering of lake sediments and peats in the chronological order of their accumulation

**stratigraphy**  the study of layering in sediments and the description of sediment profiles. Stratigraphy can provide information on the developmental sequence of a mire over time

**stratosphere**  the part of the Earth's atmosphere lying above the troposphere, from about nine to 30 miles (15 to 50 km)

**subalpine**  the zone immediately below the alpine tundra zone on mountains

**submerged aquatic plants**  freshwater plants that are rooted in soil that lies underwater and grow toward but not above the water surface, although some submerged aquatics bear flowers that extend above the water surface. Compare EMERGENT AQUATIC PLANTS

**succession**   the process of ecosystem development, which is driven by the immigration of new species, facilitation by environmental alteration, competitive struggles, and eventually some degree of equilibration at the climax stage. The stages of succession often follow a predictable sequence, and the process usually involves an increase in the biomass of the ecosystem

**tephra**   the glasslike dust particles emitted from erupting volcanoes. Layers of tephra in ice stratigraphy can serve as time markers, since the dates of eruptions are well known and the chemistry of tephra often indicates the precise volcanic eruption involved

**terrestrial**   occurring on land

**terrestrialization**   the process of succession whereby aquatic ecosystems gradually fill in with sediment

**till**   the detritus carried in and on the ice of a glacier, which is dumped as an unsorted mass when the glacier melts; sometimes called boulder clay

**timberline**   *see* TREE LINE

**topography**   the general form of a landscape, including hills and valleys

**transpiration**   the loss of water vapor from the leaves of terrestrial plants through the stomata, or pores, in the leaf surface

**tree line (timberline)**   the altitude at which general tree growth ceases on mountains, thus forming the boundary between open forest and alpine tundra. Isolated trees may survive beyond the tree line

**trophic level**   the collection of organisms that occupy a particular stage of the energy flow through an ecosystem, such as primary producer, herbivore, predator, and decomposer

**troposphere**   the lower layer of the Earth's atmosphere, up to about nine miles (15 km)

**tundra**   the open vegetation of cold, Arctic conditions, found in the polar regions (Arctic tundra) and on high mountains (alpine tundra). Trees are absent, apart from dwarf species of willow and birch

**ultraviolet radiation**   short-wave radiation from the Sun that is largely absorbed by the ozone layer in the stratosphere. It is harmful to living organisms

**uniformitarianism** the theory that geological processes such as erosion and sedimentation took place in essentially the same way in the past as they do at present. The present can thus act as a clue to the past

**vertebrate** an animal with a backbone

**vulnerability** the degree to which an ecosystem is threatened with conversion to alternative uses, such as drainage of a wetland for use in agriculture or forestry. Contrast FRAGILITY

**watershed** the geographical region from which water drains into a particular stream or wetland (equivalent to catchment). The term is also used to describe the ridge separating two catchments—literally the region where water may be shed in either of two directions

**water table** the upper boundary of groundwater in the soil

**weathering** the breakdown of rock into smaller particles in soils due to the activity of chemical, physical, and biological processes

**wetland** a general term covering all shallow aquatic ecosystems (freshwater and marine) together with marshes, swamps, fens, and bogs

**wildlife** both the wild animals and wild plants of a habitat

**xeromorphic** structurally adapted to resist drought

**zonation** the banding of vegetation along an environmental gradient, as in the transition around a shallow water body from submerged and floating aquatic plants, emergent aquatics, then to reed bed, and finally swamp

# FURTHER READING

## General biogeography

Archibold, O. W. *Ecology of World Vegetation*. New York: Chapman & Hall, 1995.

Bradbury, Ian K. *The Biosphere*. 2d ed. New York: Wiley, 1998.

Brown, J. H., and M. V. Lomolino. *Biogeography*. 2d ed. Sunderland, Mass.: Sinauer Associates, 1998.

Cox, C. B., and P. D. Moore. *Biogeography: An Ecological and Evolutionary Approach*. 7th ed. Oxford: Blackwell Publishing, 2005.

Gaston, K. J., and J. I. Spicer. *Biodiversity: An Introduction*. 2d ed. Oxford: Blackwell Publishing, 2004.

## Tundra history

Houghton, J. *Global Warming: The Complete Briefing*. 3d ed. Cambridge: Cambridge University Press, 2004.

Imbrie, John, and K. P. Imbrie. *Ice Ages: Solving the Mystery*. Cambridge, Mass.: Harvard University Press, 1979.

John, Brian S. *The Winters of the World: Earth Under the Ice Ages*. New York: Wiley, 1979.

Pielou, E. C. *After the Ice Age: The Return of Life to Glaciated North America*. Chicago: University of Chicago Press, 1991.

Roberts, N. *The Holocene: An Environmental History*. 2d ed. Oxford: Blackwell Publishing, 1998.

## The tundra ecosystem and its inhabitants

Barbour, M. G., and W. D. Billings. *North American Terrestrial Vegetation*. 2d ed. Cambridge: Cambridge University Press, 2000.

Crawford, R. M. M. *Studies in Plant Survival*. Oxford: Blackwell Scientific Publications, 1989.

Knystautas, A. *The Natural History of the USSR*. London: Century, 1987.

Sparks, J. *Realms of the Russian Bear*. London: BBC, 1992.

## Polar tundra

Aleksandrova, V. D. *Vegetation of the Soviet Polar Deserts*. Cambridge: Cambridge University Press, 1988.

Chernov, Y. I. *The Living Tundra*. Cambridge: Cambridge University Press, 1985.

McGonigal, D., and L. Woodworth. *Antarctica: The Complete Story*. London: Frances Lincoln, 2003.

Ritchie, J. C. *Past and Present Vegetation of the Far Northwest of Canada*. Toronto: University of Toronto Press, 1984.

Young, S. B. *To the Arctic: An Introduction to the Far Northern World*. New York: Wiley, 1994.

## Alpine tundra

Bowman, W. D., and T. R. Seastedt. *Structure and Function of an Alpine Ecosystem: Niwot Ridge, Colorado*. Oxford: Oxford University Press, 2001.

Hambrey, M., and J. Alean. *Glaciers*. Cambridge: Cambridge University Press, 1992.

Larson, D. W., U. Matthes, and P. E. Kelly. *Cliff Ecology*. Cambridge: Cambridge University Press, 2000.

Matthews, J. A. *The Ecology of Recently Deglaciated Terrain*. Cambridge: Cambridge University Press, 1992.

# WEB SITES

**Antarctican**

URL: http://www.antarctican.com

This Tasmanian web site carries current news from Antarctica.


**Antarctic Philately**

URL: http://www.south-pole.com

This is primarily a philatelic web site, but it contains a wealth of information on polar exploration.


**Arctic Research Consortium Austria**

URL: http://www.arctic.at

This is a good site for a wide range of links.


**Conservation International**

URL: http://www.conservation.org

Particularly concerned with global biological conservation.


**Earthwatch Institute**

URL: http://www.earthwatch.org

General environmental problems worldwide.


**Gateway Antarctica**

URL: http://www.anta.canterbury.ac.nz

This site is based in the University of Canterbury in New Zealand and has much information on wildlife and management in Antarctica.

### Glacier

URL: http://www.glacier.rice.edu

Based at Rice University, in Texas, this is a good educational site.

### The International Union for the Conservation of Nature (IUCN) Red List

URL: http://www.redlist.org

Many links to other sources of information on particular species, especially those currently endangered.

### National Park Service of the United States

URL: http://www.nps.gov

Information on specific conservation problems facing the national parks.

### Scott Polar Research Institute

URL: http://www.spri.cam.ac.uk

This is the world's leading database on the Antarctic.

### Sierra Club

URL: http://www.sierraclub.org

Covers general conservation issues in the United States and also issues relating to farming and land use.

### United Nations Environmental Program World Conservation Monitoring Center

URL: http://www.unep-wcmc.org

Good for global statistics on environmental problems.

### U.S. Antarctic Program

URL: http://www.polar.org

The site includes information on the activities of U.S. vessels in the region.

## U.S. Fish and Wildlife Service

URL: http://www.fws.gov

A valuable resource for information on wildlife conservation.

## U.S. Geological Survey

URL: http://www.usgs.gov

Covers environmental problems affecting landscape conservation.

## U.S. National Science Foundation

URL: http://www.nsf.gov

This site includes satellite images.

Note: *Italic* page numbers refer to illustrations.